THE SOULS CLOSE
to
EDGAR ALLAN POE

Graves of His Family, Friends and Foes

SHARON PAJKA

THE
History
PRESS

Published by The History Press
Charleston, SC
www.historypress.com

First published 2023

Manufactured in the United States

ISBN 9781467154543

Library of Congress Control Number: 2023934829

Notice: The information in this book is true and complete to the best of our knowledge. It is offered without guarantee on the part of the author or The History Press. The author and The History Press disclaim all liability in connection with the use of this book.

This book is dedicated to all who have helped tell the story of Edgar Allan Poe and his writing and to my father, Martin Pajka, for clipping all those news articles for me.

CONTENTS

CONTENTS

ACKNOWLEDGEMENTS

I am grateful to the prior and current staff of the Poe Museum in Richmond, including Dean Knight, Debbie Tuttle Phillips, Jaime Fawcett and especially Chris Semtner, who answered questions and shared images on behalf of the museum. Thanks to the Edgar Allan Poe Society of Baltimore, especially David F. Gaylin, for assistance. I appreciate the support of the past and present members of Friends of Shockoe Hill Cemetery, including Clayton Shepherd, Jeffry Burden and Barbara Crockett Lagasse and all the cemetery staff who were willing to guide me and share invaluable records. Thanks also to Kate Jenkins with The History Press for her feedback and assistance. Without the encouragement, support and feedback from Johnathan Shipley, this project would not have been possible.

INTRODUCTION

As a teen, I was fortunate to have grown up with a father, a daily newspaper reader, who clipped news articles about various topics that he knew I would enjoy reading. These saved articles included the annual pieces on the Poe Toaster, the name the media gave to the unidentified person who visited Edgar Allan Poe's original grave on the author's birthday for seven decades. In these articles, reporters sometimes noted freezing temperatures and how the Poe Toaster arrived regardless of the weather. Reporters always shared that the mysterious visitor left tokens of remembrance, which included three roses and a bottle of cognac. For my eighteenth birthday, a friend brought me these same tokens the Poe Toaster left, although her parents insisted that first because I was underage the cognac bottle had to be emptied. I was enchanted by the idea of a shadowy figure visiting the poet's cenotaph (an empty tomb) in the middle of the night every January 19.

I also feel fortunate having grown up near the Poe Museum in Richmond, Virginia. While I cannot recall my first visit, which perhaps was a school trip, I have many fond memories of visiting the museum, attending events and volunteering as a museum guide while I was an undergraduate student at Virginia Commonwealth University. Since that time, I have helped clean up the Enchanted Garden, shared how to make paper flowers during a gothic garden event and given lectures as a Sunday Readings speaker. One lecture, "Poe and Shockoe Hill Cemetery," connected both my love for the author and for cemeteries. I based it on my annual Poe tour in Shockoe Hill Cemetery near the anniversary of the author's death in which I highlight

Bust at the Edgar Allan Poe
Museum in Richmond, Virginia.
Author's collection.

Poe's connections to those interred in the cemetery. The Shockoe Hill Cemetery tour is significant because the cemetery includes his foster family as well as more friends and acquaintances of Poe than any other cemetery. It also is a place he visited both alone and with his wife.

In 2022, I organized a meeting at my workplace for the English department and scheduled it on Poe's birthday. I asked my colleagues to prepare to toast Poe at the end of the meeting. This led to banter with the academic dean about how Poe was a Baltimorean, which led to others noting how other cities claimed Poe. Which city or state owns Poe? The author's reach is too great to be contained to any single place. After the workplace banter, I expanded my research focus from Shockoe Hill Cemetery to finding the connections to Poe in other cemeteries. I first started in Richmond. Then I included Baltimore, since that is where Poe is buried. While researching, I discovered so many connections to the author. Because of the nature of his career as a writer, Poe connected with numerous people. The Edgar Allan Poe Society of Baltimore lists over 200 correspondents along with "420 surviving letters."[1] I also discovered that my knowledge about one of my favorite authors was somewhat narrow. I had read Poe's poems and short stories, but I had not taken the time to read and reflect on his letters or his criticism. And other than a few of Poe's works that I teach somewhat regularly in my courses, I had not revisited Poe's writing for quite a while. With all of this in mind and with my research gathered, I set out to create a grand tour of cemeteries to visit many of the people Poe knew well during his life. The names I had read in biographies and museum exhibits were now the names engraved on the tombstones.

WHY CEMETERIES?

Cemeteries are ideal places for reflection. Cemeteries remove us from the distraction of our busy daily lives. They encourage us to go within, to remember and to connect. Some of my favorite family moments have been with relatives, both living and dead, in cemeteries. I have fond memories of visiting cemeteries with my maternal grandfather, a genealogist. I also remember the first time I met my late paternal grandfather in the cemetery where my father hopes to one day be buried. Even in city cemeteries, once I step onto the grounds, I am removed from the traffic and visual reminders of the city. I silence my mobile devices. This place has my complete attention. In some ways, visiting a cemetery is like traveling back in time to see what a place looked like to people decades or even centuries ago. I discover what mattered most to them and their families through epitaphs and memorials.

Cemeteries can be seen as liminal spaces—*in-between* spaces not exclusively for the dead or for the living. Deriving from the Latin root *limen* meaning "threshold," liminal spaces are usually transitional and changing. Burial spaces that were once in the heart of the community were later pushed toward the outskirts of town only to again be "swallowed up by urban expansion," and now many of them function as green spaces with "a new range of contemporary uses [as] their principal users are no longer [only] mourners and the bereaved."[2] A focus on cemetery tourism has increased in recent years with Loren Rhoads's *199 Cemeteries to See Before You Die* and Greg Melville's *Over My Dead Body: Unearthing the Hidden History of America's Cemeteries*. In 2020, with the coronavirus pandemic, historical cemeteries with acreage to spare regained visitor attention. While indoor attractions closed to help slow the spread of the virus, cemeteries across the nation reported an increase in visitors.

Yet cemetery tourism is not a new trend. For centuries, pilgrimages have been made to burial grounds. During the Victorian era, the rise in garden cemeteries, considered our country's first public parks, offered visitors a place for respite and recreation. Poe visited cemeteries and churchyards before many of the garden cemeteries were established. He took strolls with his wife, courted women and visited and mourned late friends and loved ones.

Numerous cemeteries across the United States offer tours that make connections to some of Poe's strange tales, including Evergreen Cemetery's "Beyond the Grave: Cemetery Wanderings with Edgar Allan Poe" in Colorado Springs, Colorado; Riverview Cemetery's "Poe Walk: Morbid Curiosities" in Trenton, New Jersey; "Spirits of The Woodlands: Haunted Cemetery Tours" in Philadelphia, Pennsylvania; "The Poe Tour" in Charleston, South Carolina; and Mount Auburn's "Edgar Allan Poe Cemetery Tour" in Cambridge, Massachusetts. There are tours such as the Original Poe Grave Ghost Walk that includes a stop by Westminster Burying Ground in Baltimore, St. John's Church's "Fancy Me Mad—Tales from Edgar Allan Poe and Graveyard

Shockoe Hill Cemetery. *Author's collection.*

Tours" and the Shockoe Hill Cemetery tour that I give in Richmond, Virginia, that share Poe's connections to those interred in the burying grounds.

Some of the cemeteries that I visited were places Poe visited. For some of the cemeteries in this collection, Poe would recognize only the names on the graves, not the place itself. And for other cemeteries, Poe would recognize the names and be familiar with the land—although prior to it being established as a burial ground. I love the idea of standing where the author once stood and walking the paths he once walked. I enjoy physically being in a place associated with history—where authors walked and lived. After all, this is why historic walking tours are so popular. We want to be where history took place. There is nothing inherently unique about visiting the homes or graves of individuals whose work was admired during their lifetimes. Bibliophiles make excursions to the graves of their favorite writers. There is something unique about visiting the graves of those who were one degree of separation away from an author; although in life, people share how they may have met a friend or family member of someone famous. I wanted to meet the people Poe knew when he was alive. To do this, I conducted research and made several road trips to cemeteries.

WHY SOUTHERN CEMETERIES?

Poe was born in Boston but considered himself a Virginian, a southerner. He lived in the South most of his life and died in Baltimore while on his way to take a trip up North with plans of returning home to Richmond. Poe is credited for originating the modern detective story, developing gothic horror tales and writing the precursor of science fiction, but he worked to elevate southern literature and have it recognized. Focusing on cemeteries mostly in Virginia and Maryland, along with Washington, D.C.; Kentucky; South Carolina; and West Virginia helped me have a fuller understanding of Poe's life and the people with whom he worked, socialized, loved and even at times loathed. These were individuals who supported, inspired and challenged him. There are even a few who attempted to foil his plans.

There are several guides that focus on the houses and buildings connected to Edgar Allan Poe and those that focus on the artifacts connected to the famous author. There are also books that grapple with how the author's life and residences influenced his work. This is a book about the people who once touched the life of the author we adore. I call myself a Poe enthusiast although I have tried to accurately represent the history and the individuals in this collection. While reading his letters in which he bemoaned his situation in society and begged friends and family for money was at times daunting, I still appreciate what he was trying to do for himself and future generations—earn a living by being a writer and editor. It was a near impossible quest; arguably, it still is for many. This book includes a collection of thirty-seven memorials, nineteen cemeteries and five states, plus Washington, D.C. To have a fuller story of Poe and the people with whom he associated, I went to cemeteries and visited graves of his mother, wife, foster family, first and last fiancée, bosses, friends, cousins, school peers and instructors. I hope that this guide encourages readers of Poe to visit the cemeteries in the collection to create their own experiences with those connected to Poe.

Included in this book is a list of the cemeteries along with a brief history for each. For each personal connection, I note the cemetery and burial location and share an overview of their relationship to Poe. It is often too easy for some to walk through a cemetery admiring the memorials and epitaphs while completely forgetting that these were people with their own interests and stories. In a section called "Life Before the Stone," I share a brief biography for those included in this book. I have included

Burwell Cemetery. *Author's collection.*

a description of the grave and a section called "Grave Reflections," which includes recollections of my experience visiting the site or stories of documented visits. For cemeteries that include more than one Poe connection, readers will find a chart listing those interred in the cemetery.

THE CEMETERIES

There are nineteen cemeteries represented that are accessible to the public, since it is my hope that readers will visit the graves. The majority include a few connections to Edgar Allan Poe. Two exceptions include Shockoe Hill Cemetery in Richmond, which includes twelve connections, and Westminster Hall and Burying Ground in Baltimore, where Poe is buried, which includes five.

BLANDFORD CEMETERY is a 189-acre burial ground located in Petersburg, which makes it the second-largest cemetery in Virginia, with Arlington National Cemetery the largest.[3] With the first burial occurring in 1702, the cemetery is listed on the National Register of Historic Places.[4] The cemetery is approximately one mile from where Poe honeymooned with his young wife in 1836. *111 Rochelle Lane | Petersburg, VA 23803*

BRUTON PARRISH CHURCHYARD, located in Colonial Williamsburg in Williamsburg, Virginia, has been a burial ground since the seventeenth century. Originally, wooden crosses marked the graves, as only the wealthiest citizens could afford to ship gravestones from England. The churchyard has one of the finest collections of table tombs. The tomb that would most likely be included in a spooky Poe story is that of Governor Edward Nott (1657–1706). His stone marker with a carved skull includes popular funeral symbolism for the time signifying the curtain of life being lowered. Prominent individuals from the area were buried here, including the children of Martha Dandridge Custis, who would marry George Washington. Letitia Smith, the daughter of tenth U.S. president John Tyler is also buried here.[5] It is included on the National Register of Historic Places. A self-guided tour is available of the churchyard. *201 Duke of Gloucester Street | Williamsburg, VA 23185*

BUCHANAN EPISCOPAL CEMETERY is a small burial ground with fewer than two dozen gravestones located behind the Trinity Episcopal Church in Botetourt County, Virginia. The oldest interment, Reverend William T. Bryant, the late rector of Trinity Chapel Woodville Parish, died in 1846, just a few years before Poe's death. *19640 Main Street | Buchanan, VA 24066*

BURWELL CEMETERY, also known as Old Chapel Cemetery, is part of the land that was originally donated in 1789 by Colonel Nathaniel Burwell for Old

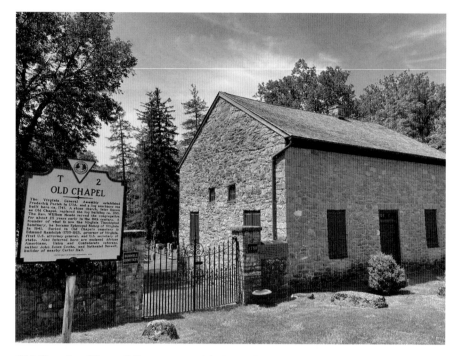

Old Chapel and Burwell Cemetery gate. *Author's collection.*

Chapel and the burying ground, which includes the grave of founding father Edmund Randolph. The stone building of Old Chapel dates from 1790. Old Chapel is on the National Register of Historic Places. *Intersection of US Route 340 and VA Route 255 | Boyce, VA 22620*

CAVE HILL CEMETERY is a 296-acre cemetery that was chartered in 1848, just one year before Poe's death. It is the largest cemetery by both number of burials and size in Louisville, Kentucky. It is included on the National Register of Historic Places. The cemetery is the final resting place of boxer Muhammad Ali and businessman Colonel Harland Sanders, known for his fast-food chicken restaurant.[6] The cemetery also includes a "poet's corner" and is the final resting place of George Keats, the younger brother of Romantic poet John Keats. *701 Baxter Avenue | Louisville, KY 40204*

CONGRESSIONAL CEMETERY was founded in 1807 as a private four-and-a-half-acre cemetery. Today, it is a thirty-five-acre cemetery located on Capitol Hill in Washington, D.C., approximately four miles from the White House, where in 1843, Poe planned a visit to meet with President John Tyler in

The Hibbs mausoleum in Rock Creek Cemetery. *Author's collection.*

hopes of securing a Philadelphia Customs House job.[7] The cemetery is included on the National Register of Historic Places. While initially known as the Washington Parish Burial Ground, the cemetery's name changed in 1830 after Congress purchased several hundred grave sites and erected monuments to members of Congress. Notable burials include David Herold, a conspirator of the Abraham Lincoln assassination, and J. Edgar Hoover, the first director of the FBI.[8] *1801 E Street SE | Washington, D.C., 20003*

GREEN MOUNT is a sixty-eight-acre historic rural garden cemetery dedicated in 1839. There are more than sixty-five thousand individuals interred here, including Abraham Lincoln assassination conspirators John Wilkes Booth, Samuel Arnold and Michael O'Laughlen.[9] Elijah Bond, best remembered for patenting what would become the Ouija board in 1891, is also buried here with a marker that resembles the infamous spirit board thanks to the Talking Board Historical Society's founder.[10] The cemetery is included on the National Register of Historic Places. *1501 Greenmount Avenue | Baltimore, MD 21202*

Green Mount Cemetery. *Author's collection.*

ELMWOOD CEMETERY is a fifty-acre municipal cemetery in Norfolk, Virginia, established in 1853. Monuments include Victorian funerary iconography such as angels, flowers and wreaths and uplifting motifs of clasped hands, emphasizing a later reconnection over a final farewell. The cemetery is included on the National Register of Historic Places. *238 East Princess Anne Road | Norfolk, VA 23510*

Elmwood Cemetery historic sign. *Author's collection.*

HEDGESVILLE CEMETERY, also known as Mount Zion Episcopal Cemetery, was established in 1881 and is located behind Mt. Zion Episcopal Church. *100 Zion Street | Hedgesville, WV 25427*

HOLLYWOOD CEMETERY is a 135-acre cemetery in Richmond that was opened in 1849 and constructed on the land known as "Harvie's Woods," which was once owned by William Byrd III, the son of the founder of Richmond. Poe played here and swam in the nearby James River when he was a boy.[11] The cemetery was designed in the rural garden style, with its name, "Holly-Wood," deriving from the holly trees that are found throughout the property.[12] Hollywood is currently one of three cemeteries that has two U.S. presidents buried there: Presidents James Monroe and John Tyler.[13] The cemetery is included on the National Register of Historic Places. *412 South Cherry Street | Richmond, VA 23220*

LOUDON PARK CEMETERY was established in 1853 with one hundred acres and is currently Baltimore's largest cemetery at nearly five hundred acres. It is the final resting place for more than 2,300 Union and 600 Confederate soldiers.[14] The cemetery is included on the National Register of Historic Places. *3620 Wilkens Avenue | Baltimore, MD 21229*

Magnolia Cemetery is a ninety-two-acre rural cemetery that rests on the banks of the Cooper River. The cemetery, which is located on the land that was the former plantation Magnolia Umbra, was dedicated in 1850. The cemetery is included on the National Register of Historic Places. *70 Cunnington Avenue | Charleston, SC 29405*

Oak Grove Cemetery is located less than a mile from the Virginia Military Institute campus. The cemetery was previously known as Presbyterian Cemetery and was renamed Stonewall Jackson Memorial Cemetery in 1863 to honor the Confederate general. In 2020, the Lexington City Council unanimously voted to rename the cemetery once again.[15] Renowned individuals are buried here, including former Virginia governors John Letcher and James McDowell, who was in office at the time of Poe's death.[16] *316 South Main Street | Lexington, VA 24450*

Riverview Cemetery is a municipal rural cemetery located on the north bank of the James River in Richmond, resting between Hollywood Cemetery and Mount Calvary Cemetery. The City of Richmond purchased fifty-three acres of land in 1887 to establish the cemetery. Opened for burial in 1891, the cemetery offers "dramatic views of the falls of the James."[17] The cemetery layout includes roundabout and meandering roads with trees dotted throughout. Today, the view of the James River is slightly obstructed in the summer due to overgrown vegetation. *1401 South Randolph Street | Richmond, VA 23220*

Rock Creek Cemetery is an eighty-six-acre park-like burial ground established in 1719 recognized for its sculptures, mausoleums and monuments. The cemetery is included on the National Register of Historic Places. There are numerous notable burials, including author and Pulitzer Prize winner Upton Sinclair; heiress Evalyn Walsh McLean, who once owned the Hope Diamond and the *Washington Post*; and socialite and photographer Marian "Clover" Hooper Adams, whose bronze sculpture seated on a granite monument is part of numerous spooky legends. *201 Allison Street NW | Washington, D.C. 20011*

Saint John's Episcopal Churchyard was the only public burial space in Richmond, Virginia, until 1822, when Shockoe Hill opened for burials. Built in 1741, St. John's is the oldest church in the city of Richmond. Poe may have attended his mother's funeral here with his new foster mother.

Magnolia Cemetery. *Author's collection.*

Saint John's Churchyard. *Author's collection.*

One of the enslaved women of his foster family occasionally would take him to visit his mother's grave.[18] There are over 1,300 burials with approximately 400 grave markers. Because of the age and condition of many of the markers, St. John's has an Adopt-a-Grave campaign where individuals can adopt a marker to help restore it. St. John's is an Episcopal church that serves an active congregation as well as a historic site for tourism.[19] There is no charge to walk the grounds of the property. A self-guided cemetery tour map is available upon request in the visitor center.[20] St. John's is included on the National Register of Historic Places. *2401 East Broad Street | Richmond, VA 23223*

SHOCKOE HILL CEMETERY was the first city-owned burial ground in Richmond, established in 1820 with the first burial in 1822. Originally known as the New Burying Ground, the cemetery is 12.7 acres and includes approximately thirty thousand interments.[21] Poe lived with his foster parents, John and Frances Allan, in several places in and around Shockoe Hill's neighborhoods. He visited the cemetery both alone and with his wife to grieve the loss of his first ideal love and his foster mother. The cemetery is included on the National Register of Historic Places. *Hospital Street | Richmond, VA 23219*

Shockoe Hill Cemetery historic sign. *Author's collection.*

UNIVERSITY OF VIRGINIA CEMETERY was founded in 1828 and serves as the final resting place for prominent individuals associated with the university as well as some students. One tragic death included the murder of student John A. Glover of Alabama in 1846 while he was attending the exhibition of Raymond & Co's Menagerie of Animals. The student tossed a burning cigar in the arena, which in turn spooked a lion and caused an uproar. The enraged trainer struck Glover with a large tent peg, which caused the twenty-one-year-old student's death.[22] In a tribute of respect, university students wore black armbands for a month.[23] Poe enrolled at the University on February 14, 1826, and continued as a student until December 15, 1826, when he left the university.[24] *Cemetery Road | Charlottesville, VA 22904*

WESTMINSTER HALL AND BURYING GROUND was established in 1787 and includes numerous renowned Baltimore residents, including politicians and war veterans. The cemetery is included on the National Register of Historic Places. Today, the cemetery is known mostly for its most famous interment, Edgar Allan Poe. Poe was originally buried in a family plot belonging to his paternal grandfather, David Poe Sr. His brother, Henry Leonard Poe, is also buried in this location. Poe's body was moved to a more prominent location

Westminster Burying Ground. *Author's collection.*

in the cemetery with a large monument. He is buried beside his aunt and mother-in-law, Maria *Poe* Clemm, and his cousin and wife, Virginia *Clemm* Poe. Beginning in the 1930s, an unknown visitor began toasting the cenotaph that marks Poe's original grave. Each year on the author's birthday, the visitor, known as the Poe Toaster, would leave three roses and an unfinished bottle of cognac as a tribute. This tradition continued until 2009. *515 West Fayette Street | Baltimore, MD 21201*

Poe's Connections

Poe's original burial place. *Author's collection.*

This book includes a collection of thirty-seven memorials, including Edgar Allan Poe's own grave site and his original grave, which now functions as a cenotaph. While it might seem that a book about Poe and cemeteries should begin with the author's own grave and cemetery, I have structured this book to include Poe's grave last because that is where the story concludes—how the author arrived in that plot. As previously mentioned, because Poe connected with a couple hundred individuals, this is not a comprehensive list. During Poe's lifetime, societal norms included home burials, so graves that are on private property or that are not accessible to the public are not included. I arranged profiles of Poe's friends, family and colleagues to introduce them during significant moments in the author's life. I followed a loose chronological order, since many of these individuals knew the poet throughout his life, not just during one particular year.

CEMETERIES BY STATE

VIRGINIA

Blandford Cemetery (Petersburg)
Hiram Hines

Bruton Parrish Churchyard (Williamsburg)
Nathaniel Beverley Tucker

Buchanan Episcopal Cemetery (Buchanan)
Edward Valentine

Burwell Cemetery (Millwood)
Philip Pendleton Cooke

Elmwood Cemetery (Norfolk)
Susan V.C. Ingram

Hollywood Cemetery (Richmond)
John Moncure Daniel
John R. Thompson

Oak Grove (Lexington)
John T.L. Preston

Riverview Cemetery (Richmond)
Susan Archer Talley Weiss

Saint John's Churchyard (Richmond)
Elizabeth Arnold Poe
Thomas Willis White

Shockoe Hill Cemetery (Richmond)
Frances Valentine Allan
John Allan
Dr. John Carter
William Galt
John McCabe
Elmira Royster Shelton
Jane Stanard
Robert Stanard
Robert Matthew Sully
Anne Moore Valentine
Elizabeth Van Lew
Elizabeth "Eliza" White

University of Virginia Cemetery (Charlottesville)
William Wertenbaker

MARYLAND

Green Mount (Baltimore)
Neilson Poe
John Pendleton Kennedy

Loudon Park Cemetery (Baltimore)
Elizabeth Herring Smith

Westminster Hall and Burying Ground (Baltimore)
Maria Poe Clemm
David Poe Sr.
Edgar Allan Poe
Virginia Clemm Poe
William Henry Leonard Poe

WASHINGTON, D.C.

Congressional Cemetery
Zaccheus Collins Lee

Rock Creek Cemetery
Rosalie Mackenzie Poe

KENTUCKY

Cave Hill Cemetery
Amasa Converse

SOUTH CAROLINA

Magnolia Cemetery
William Gilmore Simms

WEST VIRGINIA

Hedgesviille Cemetery
Joseph Evans Snodgrass

Thy soul shall find itself alone
'Mid dark thoughts of the gray tombstone—
Not one, of all the crowd, to pry
Into thine hour of secrecy.

Be silent in that solitude,
Which is not loneliness—for then
The spirits of the dead who stood
In life before thee are again
In death around thee—and their will
Shall overshadow thee: be still.

—*Edgar Allan Poe, "Spirits of the Dead"*[25]

1

Elizabeth Arnold Hopkins Poe

(1787–1811)

Saint John's Episcopal Churchyard, Richmond, Virginia
Eastern side of the churchyard near the cemetery wall
Renowned actor and mother

No earl was ever prouder of his earldom.
—Poe

Mrs. Poe was young, and she knew she was dying. Her little children surrounded her deathbed. They must have been frightened if they even understood what was happening. She handed them a jewelry box, a watercolor painting and a miniature portrait of herself. These were her most cherished possessions besides the beloved faces in the room. What dark family secrets were hidden in the letters that were left behind? The final moments were heavy, likely filled with sadness and regret. Her one relief must have been knowing that her children would be cared for.

LIFE BEFORE THE STONE

Elizabeth "Eliza" Arnold was born in 1787 to Henry and Elizabeth Arnold in London, England. While she found moments to shine, her life would never be easy. In 1789, when she was just a toddler, her father died. In November 1795, Eliza and her mother, who was an actor, sailed to the United States in hopes of a better life. After an arduous journey, the mother and daughter arrived in Boston, Massachusetts, in January 1796.

As a young girl, Eliza followed her mother's lead and became an actor, performing in numerous roles. She was an impressive young talent and stretched herself creatively. Eliza and her mother traveled down the East Coast, where they performed in Wilmington, North Carolina, and Charleston, South Carolina.[26] While the theater troupe was traveling in 1798, her mother became ill and passed away.[27] The eleven-year-old Eliza was left to be cared for by a stepfather who was considered "temperamental."[28] That same year, Eliza made her acting debut in Richmond, Virginia. She had no way of knowing that within a decade, this would be the place where she would leave her own young children motherless.

Eliza continued performing and met a fellow actor who would later become her husband, Charles Hopkins. The two performed together and were quite fond of each other. When Charles left the theater company, he headed to Virginia. Although Eliza followed the company to Philadelphia, she later returned to Virginia to be with Charles. In 1802, when Eliza was fifteen years old, the couple married.

For the next few years, Eliza and Charles traveled and performed in various cities in Virginia. Life was starting to look promising. Eliza was performing in challenging roles and building a reputation for herself, but a yellow fever epidemic would disrupt her temporary happiness. In October 1805, Charles passed away.[29]

Even as a young widow, Eliza knew that the show had to go on. She continued performing and building a relationship with another actor, David Poe Jr., from Baltimore. Born on July 18, 1784, David Poe Jr., who was three years older than Eliza, had been working as an actor and performing alongside her for a while.[30] On March 14, 1806, the two married. The marriage bond was filed in Henrico County.[31] Within nine months of the marriage, Eliza gave birth to her first child, William Henry Leonard Poe, on January 30, 1807. Eliza and David continued acting and traveling. While they were working in Boston, Edgar Poe was born on January 19, 1809. Within three weeks of giving birth, Eliza had returned to the stage.[32] By this point, David, who was said to have a "volatile temper," may have felt some jealousy when his wife's performances were favorably reviewed while his were criticized.[33] David Poe Jr. disappears from the records in the following years, although some report that he "died of consumption late in the spring of 1811."[34] A benefit was held for Eliza Arnold Poe in July 1810 in order to assist her financially.[35] Eliza's third child, Rosalie, was born in December 1810.[36] With much sadness, Eliza temporarily sent her oldest son to live with his paternal grandparents while she cared for young Edgar and Rosalie and continued performing. With declining health, possibly due to tuberculosis, Eliza continued acting until October 11, 1811, at which point she was too ill.[37] Benefits were held on her behalf since she was now without a husband and trying to care for her young children on her own.

"On this night, Mrs. Poe, lingering on the bed of disease and surrounded by her children, asks your assistance and asks it perhaps for the last time." *Enquirer*, November 29, 1811.[38]

Friends of Eliza Poe and fellow actors Luke Noble Usher and Harriet Ann Usher helped care for the Poe children while she was ill.[39] Their last name could be part of the inspiration for Poe's short story "The Fall of the House of Usher."

On her deathbed, Eliza gave her son a small watercolor painting of Boston with the inscription, "For my little son Edgar, who should ever love Boston, the place of his birth, and where his mother found her best and most sympathetic friends."[40] She had no way of knowing what a complicated relationship her young son would have with that city.

On December 8, 1811, Eliza Poe died in a boardinghouse in Richmond. Many churches prohibited the burial of actors in their churchyards, as the profession was not considered an exalted one. Accounts differ over whether it was John Allan, a prominent merchant living in Richmond who would later become Edgar Poe's foster father, or William Mackenzie, an insurance company president and theatergoer, who used his influence in order for Eliza to be buried in St. John's Episcopal Churchyard.[41] Her service was said to be held at midnight and the grave remained unmarked for many years.[42] After her death, her children were split up—William Henry was sent to live with paternal relatives in Baltimore, Edgar Poe was taken in by Frances and John Allan of Richmond and Rosalie was taken in by Jane Scott and William Mackenzie of Richmond.

The tremendous loss of a mother at such a young age affected Poe, who would later include dying young women as a literary theme in his writing.

THE GRAVE

Poe's mother's grave is in St. John's Churchyard, located on the eastern side near the cemetery wall. There is a brick walkway that leads visitors to the grave. While her exact burial spot is unknown, a memorial marks the general area of her burial. Although not seen at the grave site today, the ivy lining the Enchanted Garden at the Poe Museum is said to be taken from Eliza Poe's grave.

In 1912, the Raven Society of the University of Virginia began planning for a memorial to Poe's mother, holding a concert at Cabell Hall.[43] University students gave seventy-five dollars to start the process.[44] Although delayed sixteen years, the monument was erected to honor Elizabeth Arnold Poe thanks to the Raven Society in cooperation with the Equity Association and the Poe Shrine. When the monument was erected, Douglas Southall Freeman, the biographer, newspaper editor and author, was the master of ceremonies. The sculptor was Elbert Jackson, a notable tombstone designer along with Ernest Leland of New York, who was part of the effort and supplied the materials. The benediction was given by Reverend Hugh Sublett, the rector of St. John's Church.[45]

The memorial is a large die on base with the inscription "Elizabeth Arnold Poe" on the front. Above her name is a circular plaque that includes a profile of a woman with downturned closed eyes holding a vase with a raven flying upward. The plaque on the back of the monument reads: "The actor of talent is poor at heart, indeed, if he do not look with contempt upon the mediocrity even of a king. The writer of this article is himself the son of an actress—has invariably made it his boast—and no earl was ever prouder of his earldom than he of the descent from a woman who, although well-born, hesitated not to consecrate to the drama her brief career of genius and of beauty. Poe in 'The Broadway Journal' July 19, 1845."

The plaque on the back of the marker lists 1927 as the date, although newspaper articles show that the ceremony took place in April 1928.[46]

The grave of Elizabeth Arnold Poe. *Author's collection.*

Saint John's Church. *Author's collection.*

GRAVE REFLECTIONS

St. John's Church is one of the most significant American landmarks. Founding Father Patrick Henry gave his famous "Give me liberty, or give me death" speech during the Second Virginia Convention at this location. Today, St. John's Church Foundation offers visitors tours, reenactments, a speaker series and various special events.

In October, don't miss the Fancy Me Mad self-guided walking tour of the graveyard followed by Tales from Edgar Allan Poe in the church. In 2017, I attended this with more than a dozen friends connected to the community group River City Cemetarians, which includes individuals who visit old cemeteries together. We first had dinner at the Patrick Henry Pub and Grille and then walked over to the event. That year I remember how excited and perhaps a little shocked we were to hear the organ play *The Munsters*' theme song in the church where Patrick Henry gave his famous speech!

2

Frances Keeling Valentine Allan

(1784–1829)

Shockoe Hill Cemetery, Richmond, Virginia
Range 11, Sec. 8, Q.S. 1
Society lady and foster mother

Whenever the bureau drawers in her room were opened there came from them a whiff of orris root, and ever since when I smell it I go back to the time when I was a little boy and it brings back thoughts of my mother.
—*Poe*

Mrs. Allan had been married for eight years, and there were no children, as she was frequently ill and weak. When a local actress with little children was dying and pleaded for assistance, Mrs. Allan convinced her husband that they must foster the young Edgar Poe. She loved the boy and remained devoted to him for the remainder of her life, which sadly, was not long. Her dying wish was to see her foster son once more. Would Poe make it to her deathbed in time to say farewell?

Life Before the Stone

Frances Keeling Valentine was born on February 14, 1784, to John Valentine and Frances Thorowgood Valentine, members of the prominent Valentine family who later established Richmond's first museum.[47] In 1785, her sister Ann Moore Valentine was born. Their parents passed away by the time Frances was eleven, which could not have been far from Frances's mind when she would later take a young orphaned Poe into her home to care for as her own son. The Valentine sisters were taken in by their older half sister and her husband.[48] The girls were also fortunate to have received an inheritance from their parents, so even while times were challenging, there were financial means to support them.[49]

On February 5, 1803, Frances married John Allan, a merchant.[50] The couple resided on the corner of Main and Thirteenth Streets above the Ellis & Allan store.[51] As co-owner of the Ellis and Allan Firm, along with Charles Ellis, they exported tobacco in order to purchase merchandise including books, clothing and furniture for their shop.[52] Allan, who had emigrated from Scotland in 1795, became a naturalized citizen on June 4, 1804.[53]

In November 1811, Frances, who was without any children of her own, joined other society ladies to visit the dying actress Eliza Poe. Newspapers reported benefits being held on Eliza's behalf, as Poe's father was no longer present and his mother was left to care for her young children while ill. When the society women arrived, they found that the children were thin and pale. It was not long before Poe's mother passed away on December 8, 1811. At this point, friends of the Allans, William and Jane Scott Mackenzie, took in Poe's sister, Rosalie. The eldest son would live with his paternal grandparents, and Frances Allan implored John Allan for them to take in the toddler Poe. Together, they had no children and had financial means to support a child. Both Frances and her husband had been orphaned themselves. John Allan may have hesitated because he was supporting illegitimate children of his own.[54] It is unclear if Frances Allan was aware of her husband's indiscretions, but he did acquiesce to her request to take in the child.

Within a short period, young Poe found himself within a new household with Frances Allan doting over him. For Christmas 1811, the Allans took Poe to Turkey Island to spend the holiday. The Mackenzies stayed in Richmond and had planned to attend the theater on December 26, 1811, but canceled when young Rosalie was ill. The performance was a benefit for actor Alexander Placide and his daughter. Placide had co-starred with Eliza Poe, and this benefit had been postponed due to her death.[55]

There was a full house that night at the theater, with six hundred patrons dressed in their finest. At the start of the second act, a fire from oil lights set the stage ablaze. Chaos erupted, and within ten minutes, the entire building was blazing. Seventy-two people died, of which fifty-four women dressed in their lengthy gowns were unable to escape the building.[56] Mary Gallego, the woman with whom Jane Mackenzie had planned to attend the play, perished in the theater fire.[57]

Monumental Church was built on the site of the theater that had burned to commemorate the victims of the tragedy. A marble urn includes the names of those who passed, and the remains of the victims are in a brick crypt below the building.[58]

Detroit Publishing Co., Jackson, William Henry, photographer. Monumental Church, Richmond, Virginia, circa 1903. Photograph. *Library of Congress.*

As a young boy, Poe worshipped each Sunday with Frances Allan at Monumental Church in pew no. 80, which belonged to John Allan, who was an atheist and did not attend church. When Frances Allan died in 1829, a plaque was added to their pew as a token of remembrance.[59]

Through letters, Frances Allan is described as sickly—her illness was possibly hypochondria. In a letter to her husband on October 15, 1818, she wrote, "You are determined to think my health better contrary to all I say it will be needless for me to say more on that subject but be assure I embrace every opportunity that offers for takeing [*sic*] air and exercises."[60] The next day, she wrote:

> *I really think you have a great deal of Vanity to immagien* [sic] *you are the cause of ally* [sic] *my misery, I only wish my health would admit of my entering into all the gaieties of this place I would soon let you see I could be as happy and contented without you as you appear to be in my absence as I hear of nothing but partyes* [sic] *at home and abroad but long may the Almighty grant my dear husband health and spirits to enjoy them.*[61]

Whatever others' perception of her health, she still died relatively young at the age of forty-five. While Poe was in the military stationed at Fort Monroe, Virginia, Frances Allan died on February 28, 1829. Her dying wish was to see Poe once more. On March 2, she was buried in Shockoe Hill Cemetery. Poe arrived home the night of her funeral.[62]

Nearly two decades after his foster mother's death, Poe admitted to his friend Susan Ingram that he liked the smell of orris root, as it reminded him of Frances Allan.[63] Ingram shared, "I remember one incident that illustrates how loyal he was to the memory of those who had been kind to him." As Ingram and Poe were walking, he said, "I like it [the scent], too. Do you know what it makes me think of? My adopted mother. Whenever the bureau drawers in her room were opened there came from them a whiff of orris root."[64] There is a beautiful metaphor here regarding Frances Allan. Orris root is the rhizome of an iris, a flower as lovely and delicate as she was in life. After the bloom fades, the root is left underground for three years. It is then unearthed to dry in the sun for an additional three years. The entire process is a metamorphosis that takes approximately seven years as the root moves from darkness to light.[65] The scent is described as "earthy, flowery, peppery, musky, fresh, and velvety." Frances Allan had a loving relationship with Poe. She was one of his first teachers and a great influence on his young life. She cared about his well-being and supported his interests. He called her "Ma,"

Left: The grave of Frances Allan. *Author's collection.*

Below: The family plot of Galt and the Allan family. *Author's collection.*

and Poe recognized her as his mother throughout his life. Poe wrote, "She I believed loved me as her own child," even though the Allans never formally adopted him.[66]

The Grave

Poe's foster mother's grave is a die, base and cap that includes neoclassical elements with a rectangular pillar and an urn with a flame. Her marker is part of a family plot and is between the markers of her husband and his uncle William Galt. Her epitaph reads:

> Sacred to the memory of Frances Keeling Allan who departed this transitory life on the morning of the 28th of February 1829. This monument is erected by John Allan, her husband. In testimony of his gratitude for her unabated affection to him the zeal to discharge her domestic duties; and the fervor she manifested both by precept and example in persuading all to trust in the promises of the Gospel. Believe in the Lord Jesus Christ and ye shall be saved.

When Poe was married to his wife, Virginia, they took walks in Shockoe Hill Cemetery, where Poe would have visited his foster mother's grave.[67] The cemetery is not quite thirteen acres today but was only about four acres during Poe's lifetime.

Grave Reflections

Size matters! It is worth noting that Frances Allan's tombstone is much smaller and shorter than the markers for John Allan and his second wife, Louisa Allan. When Frances Allan died, the rights and status of women were limited. The husband was considered the head of the household, and his decisions were mostly unquestioned. While there was a family hierarchy, we often see this in the size and height of gravestones. The second Mrs. Allan's grave is the same size and stature of her husband's, most likely because she outlived him by decades. She also outlived her three sons.

Fragrant roses, daylilies and irises come to mind when I think of cemeteries. To further connect with Frances Allan and Poe's memory of her, I sought perfumes with orris root to not only stand by Mrs. Allan's grave as Poe once did but also to smell a fragrance that reminded Poe of his foster mother.

3

John Allan

(1779–1834)

SHOCKOE HILL CEMETERY, RICHMOND, VIRGINIA
RANGE 11, SEC. 8, Q.S. 1
PROMINENT MERCHANT AND FOSTER FATHER

*When I think of the long twenty one years that I have called you father, and
you have called me son, I could cry like a child to think that it should all end in
this....Why have I rejected your thousand offers of love and kindness?*[68]
—*Poe*

Mr. Allan's life was not without hardships, but he worked hard, established
himself and supported his obligations, even the offspring from affairs.
His relationship with his wife was becoming increasingly complicated. She

frequently complained about being ill. Could she have known of his marital faults? Even their foster son, whom he had supported and loved, had become an ungrateful, disagreeable teen. The death of his uncle made him a rich man, but money could not solve these problems at home.

LIFE BEFORE THE STONE

John Allan was born in 1779 in Scotland. By 1795, a sixteen-year-old Allan, who had been orphaned, immigrated to Richmond, Virginia, to work with his uncle William Galt and seek a better future for himself.[69] With Galt's help and hard work, Allan began to establish himself. Allan formed the Ellis and Allan Firm with Charles Ellis.[70] His life had changed tremendously from when he first came to the country. Allan met and courted the beautiful and kindhearted Frances Keeling Valentine; on February 5, 1803, they married.[71] The couple resided in an apartment on the corner of Main and Thirteenth Streets above the Ellis & Allan store.[72] With more attachments to his new country, Allan became a naturalized citizen on June 4, 1804.[73]

Allan's wife, Frances, was a sympathetic and loving woman who wanted to start a family. In November 1811, she joined other society ladies in visiting a local actress who was ill. That actress, Eliza Poe, had three young children who were noticeably in need of some nurturing. When the actress passed away on December 8, 1811, William and Jane Scott Mackenzie, friends of John and Frances Allan, took in the daughter of Eliza Poe. The eldest son was sent to live with his paternal grandparents, and Frances appealed to her husband to take in the toddler Edgar Poe. The couple had no children and were financially able to do so.[74] Eliza Poe did not have many possessions, but on her deathbed, she gave all she had to her children. To John Allan, she gave letters that reportedly included private family secrets that were not suitable to be shared and that were later destroyed to protect their privacy.[75] It was either Allan or William Mackenzie's influence that allowed Eliza to be buried in the churchyard.[76]

While most accounts emphasize how John Allan was not fond of Poe, early letters reveal that Allan thought a great deal of Poe as a child, calling him "a fine boy" in several letters.[77] Allan's letters mention young Poe being curious and "reading a little story book" and share his pride of the boy being a "good scholar."[78] He even complimented Poe's ability to read Latin.[79] In one letter, Allan noted that when Poe wrote, he "must direct [the letters] to his Mama" inferring the early family dynamics.[80]

While their relationship appears affectionate until Poe's teenage years, Allan's relationship with his wife was emotionally draining. Frances was constantly complaining about being ill, and her complaints and sickness troubled Allan. There were over a dozen letters noting Frances being ill and several noting that she was "complaining."[81] Although it is unclear if Frances knew of her husband's lapses, her sickness and complaints coincide with Allan's liaisons. As early as October 1812, Allan was paying for tutoring for his illegitimate son Edwin Collier. He continued paying bills for Collier until March 1818. In August 1818, Allan planned a trip to the Isle of Wight in hopes that the sea air would restore his wife's health.[82]

In 1820, Allan approached Poe's teacher Joseph H. Clarke seeking his advice about publishing a manuscript of Poe's poems. Clarke discouraged Allan from seeking publication, stating that it would be harmful "to be flattered and talked about as the author of a printed book at his age."[83]

By 1824, Allan's relationship with a teenage Poe had become complicated. Allan referred to the teen as "miserable, sulky & ill-tempered to all the family" and wrote, "The boy possesses not a spark of affection for us not a particle of gratitude for all my care and kindness towards him. I have given him a much superior education than ever I received myself."[84] Allan's household included a disagreeable teen and a frequently sick wife who complained a good amount.

In January 1825, Allan was elected to the Board of Directors of the Richmond branch of the Bank of Virginia.[85] Within a few months, his uncle William Galt, who had been Allan's closest family member since he was a teen and business advisor, died on March 26, 1825. The inheritance made Allan wealthy, but the loss of his uncle must have been a shock.

That same month, the University of Virginia opened. Allan helped Poe receive an early entrance into Thomas Jefferson's university. On February 14, 1826, just weeks after turning seventeen, Poe registered for the second session attending classes in the Schools of Ancient and Modern Languages from seven to nine thirty each morning.[86] Allan, who had worked his way up in his own career, may have perceived this as the ultimate luxury. Allan sent Poe various supplies, including clothing. Poe wrote, "The coat is a beautiful one & fits me exactly" before discussing a "terrible fight" that broke out among students, which included one student striking another with a large stone.[87] Poe's next letter to Allan discussed exams, possible degrees and even the building of the Rotunda, which was modeled after the Pantheon in Rome. Jefferson designed it to represent the "authority of nature and power of reason."[88] In this same letter, Poe concluded by discussing "a great many fights" happening among the students, including one student biting another. Poe shared, "It is likely that pieces of flesh as large as my hand will be obliged to be cut out."[89] With Poe's classmates being expelled and suspended for fighting, Allan may have been concerned that his money was being wasted with all the distractions and that Poe was "eating the bread of idleness."[90] Allan continued to send Poe money for various expenses, but the money was much less than what was required for the regular expenses of a university education, including tuition. Poe tried his hand at gambling to win a bit of money; instead, he lost and incurred more debt on top of what he had borrowed. Allan disapproved of gambling and was more than disappointed with Poe's behavior. On December 21, 1826, Poe left the university, returning to the family home, Moldavia. Allan put Poe to work as a bookkeeper. Longing for independence, Poe sought other employment, and when Allan discovered this, he denounced him as ungrateful.[91] In a March 19, 1827 letter from Poe to Allan, after they argued, Poe left home and asked for money. In an arguably dramatic ending, Poe wrote, "It depends upon yourself if hereafter you see or hear from me."[92] Allan responded the next day: "Your heart will tell you if it is not made of marble whether I have not had good reason to fear for you, in more ways than one. I should have been justly chargeable, in reprimanding you for faults had I had any other object than to correct them." Allan scoffed in his letter's conclusion, "After such a list of black charges—you tremble for the consequences unless I send you a supply of money," using Poe's "tremble for the consequences" line from his March 19 letter against him.

After Frances Allan died on February 28, 1829, she was buried in Shockoe Hill Cemetery on March 2. Poe missed her funeral, arriving home that night.[93] Allan and Poe reconnected for a short time, and Allan helped Poe obtain an appointment to West Point. Their relationship continued for a few years, although it was focused on financial means. Allan sent $100 to Poe on May 18, 1829. On May 29, Poe wrote to Allan again, requesting $100 to publish his poems. In Poe's July 26, 1829 letter to Allan, he thanked him for sending money. Poe's August 10, 1829 letter to Allan itemized his needs and expenses and asked for more money. On October 30, 1829, Poe wrote, "I am sorry that your letters to me have still with them a tone of anger as if my former errors were not forgiven." Poe requested money for lodging in his November 12, 1829 letter and then thanked Allan again for sending $80 in his November 18, 1829 letter.

On July 1, 1830, Elizabeth Wills gave birth to twins belonging to John Allan before Allan's October 30, 1830 marriage to Louisa Patterson. At this point, Allan had three illegitimate children. John Allan and Louisa's first son, John Allan Jr., was born on August 23, 1831. On October 5, 1832, their second son, William Galt Allan, was born. Allan now had male heirs to inherit his fortune.

By April 12, 1833, the father-son relationship between Poe and Allan had been completely severed. Poe wrote, "It has now been more than two years since you have assisted me, and more than three since you have spoken to me. I feel little hope that you will pay any regard to this letter, but still I cannot refrain from making one more attempt to interest you in my behalf." Poe continued, stating, "I am perishing—absolutely perishing for want of aid."[94]

On January 26, 1834, Allan and Louisa's third son, Patterson Allan, was born. That February, Poe arrived unannounced for a visit. Louisa insisted that her husband was too ill for visitors, but Poe persisted and "forced his way through the door," only to be met by Allan, who "swung his cane at him, threatening to strike him if he came any closer."[95] Allan passed away on March 27, 1834, and is buried in Shockoe Hill Cemetery. Allan's will provided for his children; Frances Allan's sister, Anne Moore Valentine, who had continued living with John Allan after her sister died; and even for his illegitimate children. He excluded his foster son from his will, and Poe received no inheritance.

THE GRAVE

Poe's foster father's grave is a die, base and cap that includes neoclassical elements with a rectangular pillar and an uncapped urn with a flame. His marker is part of a family plot and is between the markers for his first wife, Frances Allan, and second wife, Louisa Allan. All three of his sons with Louisa are buried here. His epitaph reads:

> *Sacred to the memory of John Allan who departed this life March 27, 1834 in the 54th year of his age.*
>
> *He whose remains lie buried beneath this tomb was a native of Ayreshire, Scotland.*
>
> *Blessed with every social and benevolent feeling he fulfilled the duties of husband, father, brother and friend with surpassing kindness supported the ills of life with fortitude, and his prosperity with meekness.*
>
> *A first believer in Christ and resigned to the decrees of almighty God, he gave up life with all its enjoyment without a murmur while affection*

mourns the great loss it has sustained the remembrance of his virtues and the hope of a reunion hereafter are the only sources of consolation to the bereft heart.

GRAVE REFLECTIONS

Many Poe biographers have portrayed John Allan as the villain. From my saved newspaper clippings from my father, I read that Jeff Jerome, who was the curator of the Edgar Allan Poe House and Museum in Baltimore at the time, admitted to urinating on the grave of John Allan when he first visited Shockoe Hill Cemetery.[96] Unlike other strange findings that he would point out, Dad did not underline that part of the article in his red pen. Neither of us would condone such behavior.

4

Anne Moore Valentine

(1785–1850)

Shockoe Hill Cemetery, Richmond, Virginia
Range 11, Sec. 8, Q.S. 1
Sister and Poe's "Miss Nancy"

*From childhood's hour I have not been
As others were—I have not seen
As others saw.*[97]
—Poe

Anne Valentine lived quite comfortably with her sister and her sister's husband. She cared for her sister, who was frequently unwell, and helped care for the foster child Edgar. She must have felt that she had an established place in the household, for when her sister died, she stayed and helped however she could, even when her sister's husband remarried and the new couple had children. When her sister's husband died, she received financial support from him as noted in his will and continued to remain in the home. Where else was she to go?

Life Before the Stone

Anne Moore Valentine (sometimes spelled Ann) was born about 1785 to John Valentine and Frances Thorowgood Valentine.[98] Anne and Frances's parents passed away when they were young, and they were taken in by John Dixon Jr. and his wife, who was their half sister, Sarah Valentine.[99] The Dixons' daughter Rosanna Dixon would marry William Galt, the grandson of John Allan's uncle, in 1825. The young Valentine sisters were fortunate to have a family support system and to have received an inheritance from their parents.[100] Anne never married but lived with Frances when she married John Allan in 1803.

Through letters, Anne, who is referred to as Nancy, was known to be in good health. John Allan wrote to his business partner, Charles Ellis, on August 31, 1816, noting, "Nancy weighs 146, Frances 104, myself 157 of good hard flesh—Edgar thin as a rasor [sic]." When he wrote William Galt on October 2, 1816, he shared, "Eng. Nancy is quite fat." Allan's language regarding her is always quite agreeable. Anne was healthy and pleasant, and she often cared for her ailing sister: "Nancy is so attentive a nurse, she hasn't time to visit her friends."[101] Poe frequently mentioned her in his letters home.

When Frances Allan died on February 28, 1829, Anne continued to live with John Allan in the home called Moldavia even when he married his second wife, Louisa Patterson, on October 30, 1830, and even after Allan died on March 27, 1834. In his will, Allan provided for his children, his illegitimate children, his wife and Anne Moore Valentine. He excluded his foster son from his will. Anne Moore Valentine passed on January 25, 1850, and is buried in Shockoe Hill Cemetery. Her funeral was held the next day, on Saturday, "from the residence of Mrs. Allan."[102]

THE GRAVE

Anne Moore Valentine's grave is a die and base that includes a rectangular pillar and an urn with a flame. Her marker is part of a family plot and is behind the markers for John Allan and Frances Allan. Her epitaph reads:

> *In Memory of Anne Moore Valentine who departed this life on the 25th day of Jan.y. 1850, in the 65th year of her age.*
> *Blessed are the dead which die in the lord from henceforth yea saith the spirit that they may rest from their labors and their works do follow them.*

Her marker includes a five-pointed star above her epitaph that represents Christ's divine guidance and protection. The marker also includes "Mountjoy," a maker's mark in the bottom left portion belonging to William and J. Mountjoy, stonecutters from Richmond, Virginia.

The grave of Anne Moore Valentine. *Author's collection.*

GRAVE REFLECTIONS

Although Valentine's grave is situated in the back of the family plot among the graves of the children, her marker is like Frances and John Allan's, which is a way to emphasize her relationship and status in the family.

5

EDWARD VALENTINE

(1794–1878)

BUCHANAN EPISCOPAL CEMETERY, BOTETOURT COUNTY, VIRGINIA
CROSS MONUMENT IN CENTER OF SMALL GRAVEYARD
FARMER AND POE'S FOSTER MOTHER'S COUSIN

During my childhood, you were very kind to me,
and, I believe, very fond of me.[103]
—Poe

Valentine was rather fond of the young boy his cousin had taken in as her son. When the young Poe came out to the farm, Valentine found him to be bright and curious, although he was dreadfully afraid of cemeteries. How did the young Poe come up with such ideas, and what stories were lurking in his mind at such a young age?

LIFE BEFORE THE STONE

Edward Valentine was born on February 13, 1794, to Edward Valentine and Elizabeth Singleton Valentine in Norfolk, Virginia. From 1808 to 1809, he attended Washington College in Lexington, Virginia.[104] In December 1811, his cousin Frances Valentine Allan and her husband, John Allan, took in the toddler Edgar Poe.

When Poe was a boy of five years, he visited Valentine in the western part of Virginia. Poe would ride with his foster mother's cousin to Staunton to collect letters. The town was incorporated in 1801 but would not become a transportation hub until after Poe's death. This must have been an exciting time for the young boy. On one trip, while passing a cemetery, young Poe screamed in fear. Valentine later learned that Poe had been told that "ghosts in cemeteries would grab little boys and drag them under the ground."[105]

On June 21, 1817, Valentine married Susan Archer in Norfolk while the Allans and young Poe were living in England. Their daughter Mary Eliza was born on February 13, 1818. Valentine's niece Susan Archer Talley, who would later deliver a message from Valentine to Poe, was born in February 1822 in Hanover just a couple years after the Allans returned to Richmond.

Edward and Susan Valentine remained in close contact with family members. On November 8, 1832, Valentine's father passed away in Caroline, Virginia. His mother passed on October 15, 1837.

A year before Poe's death in Baltimore, he wrote to Valentine from New York. Poe sent him a prospectus of *The Stylus*, the periodical Poe was hoping to establish. Poe had been lecturing and giving readings to raise money for the journal. In Poe's November 20, 1848 letter to Edward Valentine, he invoked the positive memories of their relationship in Poe's youth before requesting money to help with his endeavors:

> *During my childhood, you were very kind to me, and, I believe, very fond of me....I venture to throw myself upon your generosity and ask you to lend me $200. With this sum I should be able to take the first steps in an enterprise where there can be no doubt of my success* [leading to] *fortune and very great influence.*

Valentine was unable to assist Poe at the time, perhaps because that summer he had purchased land for a store and a lumber house in Buchanan, Virginia, and was making payments in installments.[106]

In the 1860s, the Valentines were living in Botetourt, Virginia. The value of his farm was $6,000.[107] Per the 1860 U.S. Census, they had $31,500 worth of real estate.

On November 12, 1867, Susan Valentine passed away after fifty years of marriage. Edward Valentine died in Goochland on May 25, 1878. He was eighty-four years old. The couple is buried in Buchanan Episcopal Cemetery.

THE GRAVE

Edward Valentine and Susan Valentine share a large cross monument in Buchanan Episcopal Cemetery, a small graveyard behind Trinity Episcopal

The grave of Edward Valentine. *Author's collection.*

Church. There are eighteen grave markers altogether, one marker belonging to their daughter Mary Eliza Valentine Jones and another to her husband, John Wigginton Jones.

GRAVE REFLECTIONS

Want to feel the chills young Poe experienced during his childhood? Take a thirty-minute drive from the cemetery to Historic Avenel Plantation in Bedford, Virginia. Avenel is a popular destination for paranormal investigators and for those who enjoy ghost tours, as it is one of the more haunted sites in the area. Considered one of the top fifteen haunted places in Virginia, hauntings include a child, a ghost cat and the apparitions of a "Lady in White."[108] The house name, Avenel, derives from a family name of characters in *The Monastery: A Romance* (1820) by Sir Walter Scott. Not so ironically, the novel includes a spirit known as the "White Lady of Avenel."[109] The property was owned by William Burwell, who was a classmate of Poe at the University of Virginia; it is believed the famous author may have visited Avenel during a trip to Bedford.[110]

6

William Galt

(1755–1825)

Shockoe Hill Cemetery, Richmond, Virginia
Range 11, Sec. 8, Q.S. 1
Prominent merchant, caregiver,
and Poe's foster father's uncle

*You will observe that the stories told are all about money-seekers,
not about money-finders.*[111]
—*Poe*

Galt emigrated from Scotland to make himself an honest businessman. By his death, he was one of the wealthiest men in Virginia. His time and energy had been focused on business. Who had time to court women? He had once loved a woman in Scotland, but she married another man—his cousin. When orphans needed a home, including the boys of the woman he once loved, he must have known he could pass down his business success to these young men and save them.

Life Before the Stone

William Galt was born in Dundonald, South Ayrshire, Scotland, on April 12, 1755, to John and Agnes Margaret *Allan* Galt. In 1775, Galt immigrated to America and settled in Virginia as a merchant.[112] Although William Galt never married, he adopted male family members from Scotland. By 1795, a teenage John Allan, who had been orphaned, had immigrated to Richmond to be taken in by his uncle William Galt.[113] Galt took the young Allan under his care and continued to be a personal and business advisor to him.

As Allan grew up, started his own business and married, he soon found himself taking in the orphaned toddler Edgar Poe in December 1811. Galt must not have found this unusual since he had taken in his nephew and would continue to take in his cousin's sons.

In 1811, Galt learned that his cousin and his cousin's wife had died in Scotland. There must have been some tension, for the cousin's wife, Jean Malcolm, had been a woman Galt had loved. Instead of marrying him, she chose his cousin instead. Now they were both gone, leaving four orphaned children. Galt must have wanted to honor her memory. On June 10, 1812, Galt wrote to one of the older boys, who was eleven years old: "You are no longer the poor orphan boy, for from thence forward I have considered you my son."[114] He made living and schooling arrangements for three of the sons, since the eldest had already gone to sea to find his own fortune.

In October 1816, as the Allans and young Poe were in England, John Allan reached out to William Galt Jr., named after William Galt's cousin, who was also named William Galt. In 1817, Galt Jr., who was now sixteen, immigrated to America to be with his adopted father. Sadly, that year, one of the other boys, Robert, who was a twin to James, passed away. James stayed in Scotland for his education until 1821, when he also sailed to America to join William Galt.

Under William Galt's generosity, his adopted family was growing and prospering. Although Allan's relationship with his own foster son, Poe, had become complicated, on September 14, 1825, William Galt's family celebrated the marriage of William Galt Jr. to Rosanna Dixon, a niece of Frances Allan. It was unfortunate that William Galt had died several months before on March 26, 1825.[115] When he died, he was one of the wealthiest men in Virginia.[116] He is buried in Shockoe Hill Cemetery.

THE GRAVE

Poe's foster father's uncle's grave is a die, base and cap that includes neoclassical elements with a rectangular pillar and an uncapped urn with a flame. His grave is among the Galt and Allan family graves and is between the markers of Frances Allan and Rosanna Dixon Galt.

Left: The grave of William Galt. *Author's collection.*

Below: The grave markers of William Galt and Rosanna Galt. *Author's collection.*

GRAVE REFLECTIONS

It is easy to make assumptions about individuals based on their epitaphs. I cannot tell you how many times I have been near William Galt's grave while visiting the Allans without understanding who Galt was as a man. He was generous with his time, training his adopted sons in his mercantile firm, and he was generous with his money. And because of the proximity of the graves near him, I had not known that he never married or had any children, other than those he adopted. Rosanna Galt's epitaph reads that she is the "late consort of William Galt." For women's graves in the eighteenth centuries, *consort* was used to mean spouse or wife of someone who had died before her husband; the term *relict* was used similarly to how we use the term *widow* today to mean that the husband died before his wife. While Rosanna Galt's grave is the same stature as Frances Allan and William Galt's is the same size as John Allan (the markers for the men being larger than the markers for the women), one might presume that Rosanna Galt, the consort of William Galt, was married to the William Galt next to her. She was married to the adopted son William Galt Jr. (1801–1851), who is buried in Hollywood Cemetery with his second wife. The William Galt (1775–1825) in Shockoe Hill Cemetery never married but took in the sons of his cousin, who was also named William Galt, and his cousin's wife, Jean Malcolm Galt. One of the children of William Galt Jr., the man buried in Hollywood Cemetery, was named William Galt (1826–1831), and he is buried behind the William Galt who is buried in Shockoe Hill Cemetery. Another child of William Galt Jr. and Rosanna Dixon Galt was Frances Allan Galt (1828–1829). Rosanna died during childbirth. Their child lived for fifteenth months and is also buried behind her mother in the Galt and Allan plot in Shockoe Hill. Her funeral was held in the home of John Allan on August 6, 1829.

7

WILLIAM HENRY LEONARD POE

(1807–1831)

WESTMINSTER BURYING GROUND, BALTIMORE, MARYLAND
LOT 27
SAILOR, POET AND POE'S OLDER BROTHER

There can be no tie more strong than that of brother for brother—it is not so much that they love one another as that they both love the same parent—their affections are always running in the same direction.[117]
—*Poe*

Separated in childhood but connected by blood and ink, Henry Poe sailed to see the world and returned home to write. What secrets were hidden behind those dark eyes? Consumed by spirits, the brothers were reunited in tragedy.

LIFE BEFORE THE STONE

William Henry Leonard Poe, commonly known as Henry Poe, was born on January 30, 1807, to Eliza Poe and David Poe Jr. in Boston, Massachusetts. He was the eldest of three children, followed by Edgar and Rosalie. After the disappearance of his father and during his mother's sickness, Henry Poe was sent to live temporarily with his paternal grandparents, Elizabeth Cairnes Poe and David Poe Sr., while his siblings remained with their mother. On December 8, 1811, Eliza Poe died, leaving Henry and the Poe children orphans. Henry returned to live and be raised by his grandparents in Baltimore, Maryland.

While living in different cities, Henry thought of his siblings. His aunt wrote to Frances Allan, who became the foster mother to Edgar A. Poe, sharing, "Henry frequently speaks of his little brother and expressed a great desire to see him."[118] The boys would continue to be separated from 1815 to 1820, when the Allans lived in England.[119] On October 17, 1816, David Poe Sr. died.

When the Allans returned to Richmond, Henry and Edgar were reacquainted. Henry visited Richmond in the 1820s, meeting Edgar's childhood sweetheart, Sarah Elmira Royster. Henry, like his brother, was inspired to write, and he even penned a story, "The Pirate," based on his brother's relationship with Royster or at least a fictionalized version.[120]

Henry was a sailor and served as a crewman aboard the USS *Macedonian*, a warship that took him to the West Indies, the Mediterranean and Russia.[121] In 1827, Henry returned to Baltimore to live with his family. It is here that he began writing poetry. In one poem, "Lines on a Pocket Book," Henry considers an accusation about his sister being illegitimate.[122] Edgar had enlisted in the army at this time, and the brothers would visit in Baltimore.

The unmarked grave of Henry Poe to the left of David Poe Sr. *Author's collection.*

Considered a "slim, feeble, young man with dark inexpressive eyes," Henry drank heavily.[123] In February 1831, Edgar left West Point and moved to Baltimore to live with his grandmother, aunt, brother and cousins. During Henry's last months alive, he would have been nursed by family members, including his brother. On August 1, 1831, Henry died from tuberculosis at the age of twenty-four and was buried beside his grandfather in Westminster Burying Ground.[124]

THE GRAVE

Henry Poe lies in an unmarked grave near his grandfather. It is covered with ivy and other vegetation.

GRAVE REFLECTIONS

While we often consider the untimely deaths of the women in Poe's life, seeing another family member, someone Poe loved dearly, die at a young age must have affected him deeply. Henry appears to have been an inspiration for his brother's writing. Some scholars believe that Poe's novel *The Narrative of Arthur Gordon Pym of Nantucket* (1838) includes autobiographical elements that point to his brother. Regardless, the two brothers were close and struggled in their existence. Considering their relationship and Henry's youthful death helps me understand how desperate Poe must have been to have a family.

8

David Poe Sr.

(1743–1816)

Gen. David Poe, my paternal grandfather, was a quarter-master general, in the Maryland line, during the Revolution, and the intimate friend of Lafayette, who, during his visit to the U.S., called personally upon the Gen.'s widow, and tendered her his warmest acknowledgments for the services rendered him by her husband.[125]
—*Poe*

David Poe knew struggle and heartache, but he came to prominence as a patriot serving in the Revolutionary War. He and his wife worked together to support their community and their children and grandchildren. During the War of 1812, he was an elder, but how could he not continue to serve his community?

Life Before the Stone

David Poe Sr. was born in 1743[126] in Ireland to John and Jane Poe and moved to Baltimore in 1755.[127] That next year, David, who was hardly a teen, lost his father. Life must have been a struggle for the young man and his family.

By 1775, David Poe had married Elizabeth Cairnes, and he was working as a wheelwright, making wooden spinning wheels and spools. Although work would have been steady, the American Revolutionary War had begun. In 1779, David Poe was called to serve in the war as assistant deputy-quartermaster general for the city of Baltimore. He attained the rank of major but was affectionately known as "General" Poe. During the war, he used his own money to help provide supplies. He was a friend of the Marquis de Lafayette, who later recounted how General Poe had given $500 to aid the troops with clothing and that his wife, Elizabeth Cairnes Poe, had "cut out five hundred pairs of pantaloons" to assist in making the soldiers' pants.[128]

After the war, David and Elizabeth Poe focused on raising their children. Their son, David Poe Jr., was born in 1784, and their daughters, Maria, born in 1790, and Elizabeth, born in 1792, followed. The family continued living in Baltimore. As David Poe Sr. focused on family, in 1802, his mother died at ninety-six.[129]

By 1805, his son had dropped out of law school to become an actor. He would soon fall for another actor, and they would have children. A family tradition included the grandchildren coming to live with David and Elizabeth to bond.[130] These grandchildren were left as orphans in December 1811. Henry, the oldest grandson, would come to stay with them. The couple must have missed Edgar and Rosalie but may have taken comfort in knowing that wealthy Richmond families were raising the children.

LAFAYETTE.

Marquis de Lafayette by unidentified artist, circa 1815, lithograph on paper, *National Portrait Gallery, Smithsonian Institution.*

In September 1814, General Poe, who was seventy-one years old and still very much a patriot, helped the Maryland Militia during the Battle of North Point, which was part of the larger Battle of Baltimore during the War of 1812. General Poe died two years later on October 17, 1816, and is buried in Westminster Burying Ground.[131]

During Lafayette's October 1824 visit to Baltimore, he visited the grave of David Poe Sr. Congress granted an annual pension of $240 to General Poe's widow.[132] There are no surviving records of Elizabeth Cairnes Poe's grave, but it is presumed that she is buried next to her husband.[133]

The grave of David Poe Sr. *Author's collection.*

The Grave

Poe's grandfather has an unornamented headstone that reads, "Burial Place of David Poe, Sr., Patriot, and Grandfather of Edgar Allan Poe, Born in Londonderry Ireland, in 1743, Died in Baltimore, October 17, 1816."

Grave Reflections

Poe would have been seven years old when his grandfather died, and he was living with the Allans in London. Poe went to Baltimore throughout his life and sought it as a place of refuge. Young Poe must have grown up hearing many stories about his grandfather's heroism, patriotism, service to the community and work ethic.

9

Robert Craig Stanard

(1814–1857)

SHOCKOE HILL CEMETERY, RICHMOND, VIRGINIA
RANGE 13, SEC. 7
LAWYER, PUBLIC SERVANT AND POE'S FRIEND

I have great faith in fools: — self-confidence my friends will call it.[134]
—Poe

Stanard knew tragedy throughout his life with the death of his mother when he was just a boy and then losing his own boys at young ages. The passing of his lifelong friend, Poe, in 1849 was another great misfortune. Like his mother's, Stanard's health had been ominous. Would a trip south restore him?

LIFE BEFORE THE STONE

Robert Craig Stanard was born on May 17, 1814, to Jane Stith *Craig* Stanard and Robert Beverly Stanard in Fredericksburg, Virginia. Stanard's father was a member of the Virginia House of Delegates at that time. Stanard was the eldest son. His brother, William Beverly, was born in 1819, and his sisters, Mary Elizabeth and Jane Stith, were born in 1822. In 1823, Stanard met Edgar A. Poe at William Burke's school in Richmond. Poe was one of the older boys in the school and was five years older than Stanard. The Stanard family lived in a mansion on Ninth Street across from the state capitol. The Allan family lived nearby on Fourteenth Street within a short walking distance.[135]

Stanard introduced Poe to his mother, who would inspire Poe's poem "To Helen." Jane Stanard, who struggled with her mental health, passed on April 28, 1824, when Robert Stanard was just a boy.[136] Her death affected him deeply, and it affected the young Poe, who was fifteen years old. Poe must have considered the untimely death of his own mother when Mrs. Stanard passed. Robert Stanard might have felt that Poe would be able to console him in a way that only a boy who had lost his own mother could.

During happier moments, in June 1824, Stanard was one of the friends present during Poe's infamous swim from Mayo's Island to Warwick Bar, a six-mile stretch down the James River. Along with their headmasters, some of the boys, including Stanard, followed the competing swimmers in a rowboat.[137] Poe was triumphant, although he had quite a bit of sunburn.[138]

The Stanard family grieved again when Robert's sister Jane passed away on October 16, 1828, when she was six years old. The emptiness in the family's large mansion must have felt vast with the loss of a mother and daughter. It would be a few years before Robert would head to the University of Virginia to start his academic career.

In May 1836, Stanard was one of the visitors who congratulated Poe and his bride on their marriage.[139] The next year, on May 17, 1837, Stanard married Martha M. Pearce from Kentucky. Their first child, Robert Craig Stanard Jr., was born on July 27, 1838, and their second son, Henry Vick Stanard, was born on September 29, 1839. Life felt hopeful and promising until tragedy struck. Henry Vick died on July 29, 1840, when he was ten months old. After such a tragedy, their son Hugh Mercer Stanard was born on September 21, 1841. Robert Stanard was elected to serve in the Virginia State Senate in 1844. He would later be a representative in the House of Delegates. Tragedy struck their household again when

Left: The grave of Robert C. Stanard. *Author's collection.*

Below: Stanard family graves. *Author's collection.*

their eldest son, Robert Stanard Jr., died in March 1845 when he was six years old.

In July 1849, Stanard saw his friend Poe for the last time as Poe was lecturing in the city. Poe had made a point to visit old friends on this trip.[140]

In 1856, after returning from a trip to Europe, Stanard's health deteriorated. During the spring of 1857, while he was a member of the convention for the revision of the Constitution, he took a "Southern tour for the benefit of his health" but died at his home on June 2, 1857, a week after returning from his trip.[141] He was forty-three years old. Stanard is buried in Shockoe Hill Cemetery.

The Grave

Stanard's grave is a die, base and cap. The epitaph on the front of the marker reads, "Robert Craig Stanard Son of Robert and Jane Stith Stanard was born at Fredericksburg Virginia on the 17th of May A.D. 1814. And died at Richmond on the 2 of June 1857." The epitaph on the side of the grave reads, "To the memory of Robert Craig Stanard the eminent jurist, the patriotic citizen, the man of honor and truth, the faithful friend, the dutiful son, the tender and devoted father and husband."

Grave Reflections

The Stanard family plot includes Robert Stanard's parents and his children. When visitors come to Shockoe Hill Cemetery, they often wish to see Stanard's mother's grave, as she was a direct influence on Poe in his youth, yet Robert Stanard was a lifelong friend to Poe. He witnessed some of Poe's infamous moments and remained a true friend until the end. After Stanard's death, his wife, Martha, went on to host the most coveted literary salon in Richmond, which attracted the "most brilliant and brainiest," including writer Constance Cary Harrison.[142] Martha Stanard was also poet John R. Thompson's "Egeria," as she was sympathetic and intellectual.[143]

10

JANE STITH CRAIG STANARD

(1790–1824)

SHOCKOE HILL CEMETERY, RICHMOND, VIRGINIA
RANGE 13, SEC. 7
MOTHER, WIFE AND POE'S MUSE

Thy beauty is to me
Like those Nicean barks of yore,
That gently, o'er a perfum'd sea,
The weary way-worn wanderer bore
To his own native shore.[144]
—Poe

Beautiful, kind and encouraging, Mrs. Stanard's words would linger with young Poe for decades. Her personage reminded him of Helen of Troy. How could she also die young? Poe's memory of her led him to perfect the flawless poem "To Helen."

LIFE BEFORE THE STONE

Jane Stith Craig was born in 1790 in Richmond to Polly Mallory Craig and Adam Craig, who had fought in the Revolutionary War and was clerk of the Richmond Hustings Court, the Henrico County Court and the General Court. She was one of six children.[145] Her father passed on May 12, 1808.[146]

In December 1811, Jane's sister, Ann Craig, who had attended the performance that had been postponed due to Poe's mother's death, perished in the devasting Richmond theater fire that killed seventy-two people.

She married Robert Stanard on February 13, 1812. Their first child, Robert Craig Stanard, was born on May 17, 1814. William Beverly was born in 1819, and Mary Elizabeth and Jane Stith were born in 1822. In 1823, her son Robert attended William Burke's school in Richmond with a classmate named Edgar A. Poe. The young Poe was a bit older than her son, but he made quite an impression.[147] Jane also left an impression on Poe. She was beautiful and intelligent, kind and encouraging. This was enough to make Poe's young heart practically swoon. Poe would later share that Jane was his "first, purely ideal love."[148] He would go on to write "To Helen" and publish it in 1831.

Scholars disagree how frequently Poe had contact with Jane Stanard. Poe's aunt and mother-in-law would later recall, "When Eddie was unhappy at home…he went to her for sympathy, and she always consoled and comforted him."[149]

Jane Stanard struggled with her mental health and passed on April 28, 1824, from "exhaustion from the mania."[150] Poe would visit her grave with his friend Robert Stanard.[151] It was also said that for months after her death, Poe would visit her grave nightly.[152]

Years later, when Poe was married, he would walk through Shockoe Hill Cemetery with his wife and tell her about his memories of Jane Stanard.[153]

THE GRAVE

Jane Stanard's grave is a die, base and cap that includes neoclassical elements with a rectangular pillar and an urn. The epitaph is quite long but mostly weathered and illegible. It begins, "To the memory of Jane Stith Standard, daughter of Adam Craig, late of the city of Richmond and the beloved wife of Robert Stanard. This monument is dedicated by the conjugal affection which retaining a fondly cherished recollection of the graces of mind and person by which it was inspired of the purity and tenderness of heart, gentleness benignity of temper the piety and virtue in which it was presented, strengthened & increased mourns with deep but resigned sorrow the sad dispensation which has consigned its beloved object to this early tomb. She departed this life on the 28th of April in the year 1824 in the thirty first year of her age."[154]

Left: The grave of Jane Stith Stanard. *Author's collection.*

Below: Poe's Helen plaque at the grave of Jane Stanard. *Author's collection.*

GRAVE REFLECTIONS

When the Poe Shrine was hosting events and openings, a plaque was added to Jane Stanard's grave that reads:

> *Poe's Helen*
> *Helen, like thy human eye there th' uneasy violets lie—there the reedy grass*
> *doth wave over the old forgotten grave—one by one from the tree top there*
> *the eternal dews do drop.*[155]

A Poe collector, John Robertson, commissioned the memorial plaque and sent dozens of violets to be planted on her grave.[156] Violets tolerate many soil types but prefer soil that is moist and rich in organic matter. Sadly, no violets remain on Jane Stanard's grave.

11

ROBERT MATTHEW SULLY

(1803–1855)

SHOCKOE HILL CEMETERY, RICHMOND VIRGINIA
RANGE 3, SECTION 5 NEAR THE CORNER OF SECOND AND
HOSPITAL STREETS
PAINTER AND POE'S FRIEND

The portrait, I have already said, was that of a young girl. It was a mere head and shoulders, done in what is technically termed a vignette manner; much in the style of the favorite heads of Sully. The arms, the bosom, and even the ends of the radiant hair melted imperceptibly into the vague yet deep shadow which formed the back-ground of the whole.[157]
—Poe

Sully honed his craft painting portraits of friends and the famous that hang in galleries and in homes. He painted two of Poe, but where are they located?

LIFE BEFORE THE STONE

Robert Matthew Sully was born on July 17, 1803, to Elizabeth *Robertson* Sully and Matthew Sully in Petersburg, Virginia. His father had been an actor in the Charleston Theater and enjoyed painting landscapes.[158] His grandparents were actors, and his father's brother, Thomas Sully, was considered one of the finest portraitists in the country.[159] It is not surprising that Sully was fond of drawing from a young age, as he was raised by creatives.

As a young boy, he attended school in Richmond, Virginia, and befriended Edgar Allan Poe. Although they were friends as young men, the Sully family had been with Poe since he was a toddler. The miniature his mother left him was painted by Thomas Sully.[160]

Robert Sully studied under his uncle for several months when he was a teen before heeding his uncle's advice and traveling to London, where he continued to study for four years. In 1828, Sully returned to the States and made his home in Richmond, where he began his career as a portrait painter.[161] Some of his recognized works include portraits of Chief Justice John Marshall, Sauk leader Black Hawk and Pocahontas from the Powhatan people.[162] Sully painted portraits for many of the women in Poe's life, including his foster mother, Frances Allan; his sister's foster mother, Jane Scott Mackenzie; and Virginia Clemm.[163]

On December 11, 1832, Sully married Isabella Jerdone Thompson.[164] While the couple had five children together, they were "unsuited" for each other, and his wife moved with her children to Culpepper, Virginia, in the 1840s.[165]

In May 1836, Sully was one of the friends who congratulated Poe and Virginia Clemm on their marriage.[166]

Poe and Robert Sully had some influence on each other's works—Sully painted a young woman's portrait and placed it in an oval frame, which may have inspired Poe's short story "The Oval Portrait," although scholars note the name "Sully" in the piece references Thomas Sully.[167] Robert Sully also painted an illustration of Poe's poem "Lenore." Accounts differ whether Poe saw the completed work.[168]

The grave of Robert Matthew Sully. *Author's collection.*

In July 1849, Sully saw his friend for the last time during Poe's lecture tour.[169] That October, Sully grieved Poe's death.[170]

In September 1854, Sully, who was deeply concerned with the preservation of Virginia's history, traveled to Jamestown to paint the ruins of the old church. His October 1854 letter to Lyman Draper, a historian who served as the secretary for the State Historical Society of Wisconsin, details his findings in hauntingly macabre descriptions. Sully depicted Jamestown as "far more romantic, than agreeable":

> *I have seen many a ruin in many a land but…never did I behold a scene of such funereal solitude. The death like, unbroken silence—Bird and even insect have forsaken the spot. You are alone among the dead. The light, playing through the arch casting a dim reflection, in the broken tombs, the massive trees hemming in & enclosing the whole, is endeed [sic] a Picture.*[171]

Sully continued working in Richmond until 1855. After painting several portraits for the State Historical Society of Wisconsin, he was elected an honorary member of the society and that October headed to Madison, where he planned to visit and settle in the area.[172] While on his way, he died in Buffalo, New York, on October 28, 1855.[173] In the confusion surrounding his sudden death, his papers and baggage were lost.[174]

Sully is buried in Shockoe Hill Cemetery.

THE GRAVE

Sully's headstone is seemingly plain for an artist. His epitaph reads, "Our brother Robert M. Sully Died October 30th 1855.[175] There is rest in heaven."

GRAVE REFLECTIONS

Not far from Sully's grave is that of John Marshall (1755–1835), who served as a U.S. congressman, the secretary of state and a Supreme Court Justice. Marshall continues to be the longest-serving chief justice and fourth-longest-serving justice in U.S. Supreme Court history.

12

Nathaniel Beverly Tucker

(1784–1851)

Bruton Parish Cemetery, Williamsburg, Virginia
West of the walled entrance to the churchyard
Legal scholar and author whose work was admired by Poe

*I would be proud if you would honor me frequently with your criticism.
Believe me when I say that l value it.*[176]
—Poe

Beverly Tucker was frustrated by the politics of the day, but like Poe, he also wrote poetry, essays and criticism for the *Southern Literary Messenger*. Poe admired Tucker's work and was touched on learning that Tucker had met his mother. Could either of these men imagine that Tucker's novel predicted the future—the Civil War?

Life Before the Stone

Nathaniel Beverly Tucker was born on September 6, 1784, in Chesterfield County, Virginia, to St. George Tucker and Frances *Bland* Randolph Tucker. Tucker's father came to Virginia in 1771 to attend the College of William & Mary studying under George Wythe. When Tucker was just a toddler, his mother died.[177] In 1791, his father married, and while his stepmother was kind, the family struggled, as more than half of Tucker's siblings died before he was twelve.[178] His older brother, Henry St. George Tucker, who would become a U.S. congressman and serve as a Virginia State Court judge, was studious and encouraged the young Beverly to follow suit. In 1799, Beverly enrolled at William & Mary. His undergraduate studies ended in 1802, when students rioted over the expulsion of students caught dueling. Tucker's father sent him to Staunton, Virginia, to study law.[179]

In 1809, Tucker began practicing law, and on February 9, 1809, he married Mary Coalter. The couple would have four children. In 1816, he moved the family to Missouri, where he would live for seventeen years. His wife died in 1827, but he married again. In 1832, he returned to Williamsburg. It was during this period in the 1830s that Tucker began writing poetry, essays and book reviews for the *Southern Literary Messenger*.[180] Tucker had met Poe's mother when she was a young actress. Poe wrote:

> *In speaking of my mother you have touched a string to which my heart fully responds. To have known her is to be an object of great interest in my eyes. I myself never knew her—and never knew the affection of a father. Both died (as you may remember) within a few weeks of each other....The want of parental affection has been the heaviest of my trials.*"[181]

Poe valued Tucker's criticism and Tucker saw Poe for his genius. While working as a law professor, Tucker wrote novels—*The Partisan Leader* in 1836; and *George Balcombe*, also published that year, was called "the best American novel" by Edgar Allan Poe.[182] Tucker published his novel *Gertrude* in the *Messenger* between 1844 and 1845.

Tucker died on August 26, 1851, at age sixty-six. He is buried in Bruton Parish in Williamsburg, Virginia.

THE GRAVE

Tucker's grave is an obelisk that is in the bricked sidewalk portion of the churchyard. The epitaph reads:

> *Sacred to the memory of Judge Nath Beverly Tucker Born 6th September AD 1784 Son of St. George Tucker President of the Court of Appeals of Virginia and Frances Bland Died August 26th AD 1851 And of his wife Lucy Ann Tucker Born November 11th AD 1812 daughter of Gen. Thomas A. Smith US Army and Cynthia B White Died February 18th AD 1867.*

The side of the marker reads:

The grave of Nathaniel Beverly Tucker. *Author's collection.*

Descended from Virginia's best blood
Judge Tucker
Was by birth, and training, a gentleman of the old school
He filled with credit and distinction positions of trust
and dignity. Was Judge of the U.S. Court in
the Territory of Missouri, and after his return
to his native State was the Professor of Law
in the College of William and Mary till his death
His influence in developing the minds and characters
of his pupils was a prominent trait in his character
He was a ready, accurate, and elegant writer
He was hospitable, benevolent, and charitable
And his honor and integrity were without a stain
This eminent scholar and author; upright Judge
learned jurist, constant friend, affectionate husband
and Father died as he lived, a Sage, a Patriot
and a Christian.

The grave also includes the maker's mark for "Wallen & Wray, Rich'd."

Grave Reflections

My husband and I have spent our vacations in Colonial Williamsburg for over a decade. Bruton Parish Cemetery is a place that we visit frequently, partly because the trees provide shade and the brick walls provide a bit of distance from the hectic crowds of tourists. Tucker's marker is significant for more reasons than a lasting memory to the man. His daughter organized the Catherine Memorial Society in 1884, named after her daughter and Judge Tucker's granddaughter, in order to preserve gravestones in Bruton Parish. This is considered the first organized restoration movement in Williamsburg.[183]

13

WILLIAM WERTENBAKER

(1797–1882)

UNIVERSITY OF VIRGINIA CEMETERY, CHARLOTTESVILLE, VIRGINIA
NEAR EASTERN WALL OF THE OLDER SECTION OF THE CEMETERY
LIBRARIAN AND CONFIDANT TO THE YOUNG SCHOLAR, POE

*There lives no man who at some period has not been tormented, for example,
by an earnest desire to tantalize a listener by circumlocution.*[184]
—*Poe*

He had only been librarian for mere weeks when young Poe sought French books. The young poet made quite an impression on Wertenbaker, especially on that cold and dark December night when, with some tallow candles, Poe shared his regrets. Wertenbaker carefully catalogued Thomas Jefferson's books for the library. Could he have believed that Jefferson would remember him?

LIFE BEFORE THE STONE

William Wertenbaker was born on June 1, 1797, in Milton, in Albemarle County, Virginia, to Christian Wertenbaker and Mary O'Grady Wertenbaker.[185] His family emigrated from Swibrechen, Germany, to Maryland before moving to Virginia. His early life included working at the clerk's office in Albemarle.

When Wertenbaker was a teen, he volunteered to serve in the Virginia militia during the War of 1812. He was a private in the Eighth Regiment under the leadership of General John Hartwell Cocke, a brigadier general. Wertenbaker received a pension until his death.[186]

Wertenbaker was at work when he first met Thomas Jefferson. About 1816, Jefferson entered the clerk's office of the Albemarle County Courthouse, where Wertenbaker was copying deeds. He assisted Jefferson when both men realized there was no one there to help the former president. Jefferson asked for the clerk and his deputy, but both had left for dinner. Although Jefferson must have been displeased by the situation, Wertenbaker was able to supply him with his necessary records, and as Jefferson was leaving, he stated, "I will not forget you."[187]

Wertenbaker enrolled at the University of Virginia as a student of law in 1825. In 1826, while a student, he was appointed librarian by Thomas Jefferson, who indeed had not forgotten the former young man who had assisted him in the clerk's office nearly a decade before.[188] He received his commission from Jefferson on January 30, 1826, written in his own handwriting.[189] The document was framed and hung in the library for many years.[190]

Wertenbaker became librarian just two weeks before Edgar A. Poe enrolled in the second session of classes on February 14, 1826.[191] Wertenbaker would later share a story in which one of Poe's professors "requested his Italian class to render into English Verse a portion of the lesson in Tasso, which he had assigned them for the next lecture." Pointing to a studious Poe, Wertenbaker further recalled, "At the next lecture on Italian, the Professor stated from his chair that Mr. Poe was the only member of the class who had responded to his suggestion, and paid a very high compliment to his performance."[192] Wertenbaker's recollections noted that Poe was held in high regard by faculty. He was "an intelligent and polished gentleman."[193] Wertenbaker was also there on that "cold night in December" when Poe realized he had incurred a $2,000 gambling debt. Poe spoke of regret and insisted that he would pay back the balance he owed.[194] Poe left the university on December 15, 1826.[195]

In 1828, under Wertenbaker's charge, the first printed catalogue of the University of Virginia Library was released and listed approximately eight thousand titles.[196] Wertenbaker was the last survivor of all who were connected with the university at its establishment and directly connected with Thomas Jefferson. During Jefferson's last visit to the university, he had an appointment with Wertenbaker.[197]

On September 2, 1829, Wertenbaker married Louisiana Timberlake. While the couple must have looked forward to starting a family and building their lives together, Wertenbaker's father passed in 1833. Tragedy would continue, as the couple outlived two of their three sons. Their daughter,

Mary LeTellier, was born in 1840, just one year before their oldest son passed away. Wertenbaker devoted much of his life to the Presbyterian church and was elected an elder in 1844.[198]

Their third son, Thomas O'Grady, died in 1862. He was a soldier in the Civil War and died while on retreat from Williamsburg. They had hoped that their son would enter the Presbyterian ministry before his death.[199] Also during the time of the Civil War, Wertenbaker's mother passed in 1864.

In 1868, Wertenbaker published his recollections of Poe in the November-December issue of the *Virginia University Magazine*.[200]

The couple faced many hardships but were also able to celebrate a golden wedding anniversary in September 1879.[201] Just prior to their anniversary, Wertenbaker was paralyzed that March but continued working as a librarian. The university's Board of Victors voted to give him pay for the remainder of his life and appoint an assistant. In 1880, the honor of emeritus librarian was bestowed on him.[202]

Wertenbaker died on April 7, 1882, and is buried at the University of Virginia Cemetery.

THE GRAVE

William Wertenbaker's grave is a die on base that reads, "William Wertenbaker June 1, 1797 / April 7, 1882 / Librarian of the University of Virginia / By Appointment of / Thomas Jefferson / January 30, 1826."

The War of 1812 Society in Virginia also listed Wertenbaker on a plaque at the entrance of the cemetery that was placed in 2006. This plaque also includes George Tucker (1775–1861), a professor who influenced Poe and who also submitted his writing to the *Southern Literary Messenger*.[203]

GRAVE REFLECTIONS

The University of Virginia Cemetery is the only cemetery that I have ever gotten in trouble for visiting. Growing up with a grandfather as a genealogist, cemeteries were part of our trips to family reunions. It was not until I was a high schooler attending the UVA Young Writers Workshop, a residential summer program offering studio workshops for teens, that I understood people's complicated relationships with burial grounds. While a good amount of time of the program was working with

Left: The grave of William Wertenbaker. *Author's collection.*

Right: War of 1812 plaque. *Author's collection.*

other young writers and instructors, the program included built-in free time for a writer to produce content. My roommate was quite social, so I sought a place that was both quiet and that offered a way to commune with nature to work on one of my assignments. We were forbidden from crossing the street alone, but the old cemetery was much too tempting. With my flute in hand, I looked both ways and entered the sacred grounds to work on lyrics for a song. Evidently, someone told on me, because when I returned, I was reprimanded by the counselor, whom I now realize was merely a young college student. While she understood my need for solitude, she scolded me for entering the cemetery, as it was "dangerous" to enter alone. Over thirty years later, I still recalled that scene when entering the University of Virginia Cemetery. The only danger I noticed were the large tree roots that one could trip over if not careful.

Not far from Wertenbaker's grave is that of George Tucker, an influential professor from the University of Virginia, as well as Basil Lanneau Gildersleeve (1772–1834), a classical scholar and educator who had heard Poe speak and recite "The Raven" at a hotel in Richmond, Virginia, in Gildersleeve's youth. Gildersleeve recalled Poe's "voice was pleasant....He

Above: The grave of Basil Lanneau Gildersleeve. *Author's collection.*

Right: Basil Lanneau Gildersleeve portrait. *George Grantham Bain Collection, Library of Congress Prints and Photographs Division.*

was sensitive to the music of his own verses; and that was the element he emphasized in his delivery."[204]

With themes of reincarnation and mesmerism, read Poe's "A Tale of the Ragged Mountains" and then drive five miles from the cemetery just southwest of Charlottesville to experience the group of hills known as the Ragged Mountains (1730 Reservoir Road | Charlottesville, VA 22903).

14

John T.L. Preston

(1811–1890)

Oak Grove Cemetery, Lexington, Virginia
Plot # 19
Founder of Virginia Military Institute and
classmate of Poe

*You will learn to judge for yourself of what is going on in the world,
without trusting to the gossip of others. Believe nothing you hear,
and only one half that you see.*[205]
—*Poe*

The colonel looked back decades to remember the childhood friend who
became the world-famed poet. He remembered their schooling and
young Poe's poetry. Would dark shadows enter his mind? This was the calm
before the storm.

LIFE BEFORE THE STONE

John Thomas Lewis Preston was born on April 25, 1811, in Lexington,
Virginia, to Thomas Lewis Preston and Edmonia Madison *Randolph*
Preston. His early education was in Richmond, Virginia, where he met
a young Edgar Poe. Preston would later recall, "Poe was the swiftest
runner, the best boxer, and the most daring swimmer at Clarke's school,"
referencing the school under headmaster John Clarke of Trinity College,
Dublin.[206] Preston was one of the younger boys at the school while Poe
was one of the oldest, so it is not too surprising that his recollections feel
extravagant. He admired Poe's athletic ability and was "captivated" by his

strength. He recalled that Poe "would allow the strongest boy in the school to strike him with full force in the chest." In addition to great athleticism, Preston noted Poe was an excellent scholar, "yet with all his superiorities, he was not the master-spirit, nor even the favorite of the school."[207] Preston admired Poe's writing so much that he asked if he could bring it home for his mother to read; he argued she was Poe's "first critic," as she had "a natural love for literature."[208]

Afterward, Preston attended Washington College, where in 1828 he received his bachelor of arts degree. Preston also attended graduate courses at the University of Virginia. He later studied law.

In 1832, Preston married Sarah Lyle Caruthers. The couple had seven children. In 1836, after Preston made a case that the Lexington arsenal could be transformed into a normal school providing education and military training, the Virginia legislature passed a bill to put this into action.[209] Preston then served on the new school's board and was tasked with naming the school, which he named Virginia Military Institute.[210] By 1839, the school had been set up, and Preston applied to become a faculty member, serving as a Latin professor.

When their youngest son was just a few years old, Sarah died. Preston had met Margaret Junkin, who was the daughter of Washington College's former president. She would become a renowned writer known as the "Poetess of the South." In 1857, they married. The year before, Junkin had published *Silverwood: A Book of Memories*, "an exploration of the clash between traditional values of honor and family and the new market economy that was sweeping through the United States and the Shenandoah Valley."[211]

In 1859, Preston observed the execution of John Brown, an abolitionist who led a raid on the federal armory at Harper's Ferry, as part of VMI's Corps of Cadets. During the Civil War, Preston fought on the side of the Confederate States, although he was active in the Presbyterian Church and helped lead Sunday school classes for free and enslaved African Americans before the war.[212] After the war, he returned to VMI, where he taught until retirement in 1881.[213]

Preston died on July 15, 1890, and is buried in Oak Grove Cemetery.

THE GRAVE

Preston's grave is a die in socket. The epitaph includes his name, John T.L. Preston, on the top of the marker. On the table, it reads "April 25,

The grave of John Preston. *Author's collection.*

1811–July 15, 1890. An officer of the Commonwealth, of the Confederate States, and the Church of Christ. He fought a good fight. He finished his course. He kept his faith. Laus Deo."[214]

GRAVE REFLECTIONS

This was my second time visiting Oak Grove Cemetery. The first time, I visited Preston's wife, author and poet Margaret Junkin Preston, who was considered a Southern war poet best known for her works *Beechenbrook: A Rhyme of War* (1865), *Old Song and New* (1870) and *Aunt Dorothy: An Old Virginia Plantation Story* (1890).[215] This trip let me reconnect with her again by reading letters connected to the Poe Memorial. Sarah S. Rice, a Baltimore school teacher who organized the efforts to provide a memorial for Poe's grave through her "pennies for Poe" campaign, wrote to Margaret J. Preston requesting a poem for the inauguration of the memorial on November 25, 1875. In the response letter from October 8, 1875, Margaret J. Preston remarked that her husband "was a boyish friend of Poe's when they went to school together in Richmond; who used to sit on the same bench with him, and together with him pore over the same pages of Horace." She continued, "To him as his earliest literary critic—a boy of fourteen—Poe was accustomed to bring his first verses. Even then, youth as he was, he was distinguished by many of the characteristics which marked his after life."[216] The letter was written in Lexington, just miles from where I stood in the cemetery. Reading such letters while standing in cemeteries connects me to history.

15

John Collins McCabe

(1810–1875)

Shockoe Hill Cemetery, Richmond, Virginia
Range 5, Sec. 6
Clergyman, writer and friend of Poe

*I feel exceedingly desirous that you should be even more favorably known
to the public than you are at present.*[217]
—*Poe*

Reverend McCabe was a man of letters who contributed writing to church journals and literary newspapers, including the *Southern Literary Messenger*. His work was ephemeral, paralleling the tragic loss of several wives. In times of disease and turmoil, would this love last?

Life Before the Stone

John Collins McCabe was born on November 12, 1810, to William McCabe and Jane *Collins* McCabe in Richmond, Virginia. He studied medicine but entered banking for his profession before becoming a clergyman.

He married Emily Agnes Hardaway. Their first daughter, Mary, was born on January 10, 1831, but died on July 7, 1832. Their daughters Emma Agnes and then Jane were born a few years after. While balancing work and home, McCabe found time to compose poetry. A collection of poems titled *Scraps* was published in 1835.[218] Although life seemed promising, on July 18, 1837, McCabe's wife passed away.[219] He was left with two young girls.

By this time, McCabe had befriended Edgar A. Poe, who was serving as editor of the *Southern Literary Messenger*. Although Poe admired McCabe's work and considered him a friend, editors must make tough decisions when considering their magazines. On March 3, 1836, Poe rejected McCabe's poem "The Consumptive Girl," calling it "deficient" and "rough" because of McCabe's "frequent choice of words abounding in consonants."[220]

On August 7, 1838, McCabe married Eliza Sophia Gordon Taylor. Their son William Gordon was born on August 4, 1841. In 1845, McCabe became an Episcopal minister. Their daughter Virginia was born in 1849. McCabe continued to submit writing to the *Southern Literary Messenger*, now under the editorship of John R. Thompson. On July 15, 1850, their daughter Elmina Isabelle was born. He served as a rector of the Church of the Ascension in Baltimore and later as the rector of Saint Anne's Parish in Middleton, Delaware.[221]

Reverend McCabe was included in Poe's 1841 "Chapter on Autography," which is considered a work of graphology. Printed in *Graham's Magazine*, Poe analyzed the handwriting of literary figures of the time to determine their personality traits. This may have included more literary criticism than actual handwriting analysis. For John McCabe, Poe asserts McCabe's writing "is in every respect a bad one—an ordinary clerk's hand, meaning nothing. It has been strongly modified, however, by circumstances which would scarcely have permitted it to be otherwise than it is."[222]

After Poe's death and just before the Civil War, McCabe received an honorary doctor of divinity degree from the College of William & Mary in 1859. His second wife passed in 1861. During the Civil War, he returned to Richmond, traveling through the Union blockade to become chaplain of the Thirty-Second Virginia Infantry Regiment. McCabe's daughter Jane from his first marriage died on February 16, 1862. Within a few months, he married Marie V. DeFord on May 15, 1862.[223] He was later appointed as the chaplain general of Richmond's prisoner-of-war facilities, including Libby Prison. He continued in this position until the end of the war. Shortly after the war, on July 17, 1867, Marie passed away.

On September 15, 1868, McCabe married Virginia Mackall.[224] The couple had one son, Henry Clinton.[225] McCabe died on February 26, 1875, while in Pennsylvania. McCabe is buried in Shockoe Hill Cemetery in Richmond.

Right: The grave of John Collins McCabe. *Author's collection.*

Below: The graves of John Collins McCabe and Emily Hardaway McCabe. *Author's collection.*

THE GRAVE

McCabe's headstone includes an engraved cross passing through a crown, a Christian symbol of the reward in heaven deriving from the trials in life. The epitaph reads, "In memory of Rev. John Collins McCabe D.D." with his birth and death dates. "At Rest" is centered at the bottom of the marker. He is buried next to his first wife, although a tree has grown between them.

GRAVE REFLECTIONS

Poe rejected McCabe's poem "The Consumptive Girl" but noted that "it breathes the true spirit of poetic sentiment and feeling—it has fine and original images—and has the proper material of the Muse." I cannot help but wish that I could read the poem.

16

Rosalie Mackenzie Poe

(1810–1874)

Rock Creek Cemetery, Washington, D.C.
Section D, Lot 29, Grave 2
Penmanship instructor and Poe's sister

*Rosalie is still living at Mr. McKs still unmarried,
and is treated as one of the family, being a favourite with all.*[226]
—*Poe*

Life Before the Stone

Rosalie Poe, who was frequently called Rose, was born in late December 1810 in Norfolk, Virginia, to Eliza Poe and David Poe Jr., although there were speculations that she was Edgar and Henry's half sister.[227] After the disappearance of her father, society women arrived to find the Poe children thin and pale. Rosalie was much too young to remember any of this or even the death of her mother on December 8, 1811, but on her mother's deathbed, she was given a jewelry box.[228] William and Jane Scott Mackenzie took in the baby Rosalie, while her eldest brother, Henry, would live with his paternal grandparents and Frances and John Allan would take in the toddler Edgar Poe. Until she was ten, Rose believed that Jane Mackenzie was her birth mother.[229] Rose had been quite sick as a child. During Christmas, the Mackenzies had planned to attend the theater on December 26, 1811, but canceled when their new foster daughter was ill. This may have saved Ms. Mackenzie's life, as this was the night of the Richmond theater fire. Within ten minutes of the start of the fire, the entire building was blazing. In total, seventy-two people died, including fifty-four women dressed in evening gowns who were unable to escape the building.[230] Mary Gallego, the woman with whom Jane Mackenzie had planned to attend the play, died in the theater fire.[231]

Rose was baptized as Rosalie Mackenzie Poe. Being raised in a household of means, Rose had many privileges and was given the finest opportunities to be educated so that she could one day work at the girls' school run by the Mackenzie family.[232] In June 1815, Edgar Poe moved with the Allans to England, where they would remain until July 1820. Rose would later say that she was not aware of having brothers until she was "a good sized girl."[233] While her brothers grew in their intellects, "some mysterious blight had fallen upon [Rose]," and she "gradually drooped and faded into a languid, dull and uninteresting girlhood—apathetic in disposition and weak in body and mind."[234]

By her mid-twenties, Rose taught penmanship at the Mackenzie school. While she had excellent handwriting and oversaw writing the bills, she would weep without reason.[235] One student recalled that Rose had some odd behaviors and would stare out the window for long periods of time.[236]

By the summer of 1848, the Mackenzie school had closed and Rose no longer worked. While just in her late thirties, she dressed unfashionably and had noticeable wrinkles that made her look older than she was.[237] The next year proved to be an exciting time for her, as it was Edgar Poe's 1849 summer lecture tour. She reconnected with her brother, and together they visited friends around Richmond.[238] Along with some friends, Rose and Mrs. Mackenzie attended Poe's Richmond lecture on August 17, 1849, and again Rose attended his lecture on September 24, 1849. During this second lecture, Elmira *Royster* Shelton, Poe's childhood sweetheart with whom he was reconnecting, was in the audience.[239] Rose followed Poe around the city and would sometimes go with him when he visited Shelton at her home.[240]

Rose loved beauty; she found it in her brother's poetry, especially "The Raven" and "The Bells," which were said to be her favorites. She once shared, "I often feel as if I could write poetry. I have it all in my head, but somehow can't get it clear enough to write down."[241] Like her brother, she also had a love for flowers. A friend shared, "I rarely saw [Edgar Poe] without some delicate bud or leaf in his buttonhole, and a bouquet was his sister's constant accompaniment."[242]

After Edgar and his wife, Virginia, died, Rose sent her savings to her aunt, Maria Clemm, who was soliciting charity after the death of her daughter and son-in-law, even though Rose once recalled, "I don't remember that Aunt Clemm ever spoke a kind word to me."[243] In 1849, Rose lived comfortably with the Mackenzies. When her brother died, she did not seek the rights to Edgar Poe's writing; she cared more about her sentimental attachment to his trunk.[244]

Rose lived with the Mackenzies until after the Civil War, when the family lost everything like many other Virginians. On hard times, Rose stayed in Richmond until she could make her way to Baltimore, where she had hoped relatives would aid her. They did not. By the age of sixty, she was homeless and alone. Rose tried to support herself by selling photos of her famous brother. She also reached out to people who once knew or admired her brother, asking for charity.[245]

At sixty-four, with failing health, Rose entered Epiphany Church Home, a charity shelter in Washington, D.C. On July 21, 1874, as she was picking up a charitable gift from a Poe admirer who had sent her money, she passed away. She was interred in a pauper's plot in Rock Creek Cemetery that belonged to the shelter.[246]

THE GRAVE

Rosalie Mackenzie Poe is buried almost in the middle of the churchyard just northeast of the church. She has a raised top gravestone that reads, "Rosalie Mackenzie Poe / 1812–1874." The birth year should be 1810.

The grave of Rosalie M. Poe. *Author's collection.*

Rabboni by artist Gutzon Borglum. *Author's collection.*

GRAVE REFLECTIONS

Although buried in a pauper's plot, Rose's grave is in a gorgeous part of Rock Creek Cemetery. Just feet away is the bronze sculpture *Rabboni* by artist Gutzon Borglum that depicts Mary Magdalene emerging from an alcove after Jesus has risen from his tomb.

Rose's foster mother, Jane *Scott* Mackenzie, is buried in Shockoe Hill Cemetery in an unmarked grave.

John Hamilton Mackenzie (1806–1875) is buried in Grove Street Cemetery (940 Grove Street | Danville, VA 24541), 253 miles from Rose's burial plot. Grove Street Cemetery is the first municipally owned burial ground in Danville, Virginia, with the first known interment dating 1833.[247] John Hamilton Mackenzie was Rose's legal guardian after her foster father, William Mackenzie, died and left her destitute, even though she had received a $2,000 inheritance from Joseph Gallego, a wealthy Richmonder who owned a flour mill.[248]

17

JOHN PENDLETON KENNEDY

(1795–1870)

GREEN MOUNT CEMETERY, BALTIMORE, MARYLAND
LOT M, 32-24
U.S. CONGRESSMAN, AUTHOR AND POE'S FRIEND

You gave me my first start in the literary world, and since indeed I seriously say that without the timely kindness you once evinced towards me, I should not at this moment be among the living—you will not feel surprise that I look anxiously to you for encouragement in this new enterprise.[249]
—*Poe*

K ennedy had worked his way up in literary society and was a member of the Delphian Club. He once advised Poe to "rise early, live generously, and make cheerful acquaintances,"[250] but such instruction was not exactly what the young writer needed. Did Poe need a patron?

LIFE BEFORE THE STONE

John Pendleton Kennedy was born on October 25, 1795, in Baltimore, Maryland, to John Kennedy, a merchant and Irish immigrant, and Nancy *Pendleton* Kennedy, a descendant of one of the First Families of Virginia. Kennedy attended private schools and then the Baltimore Academy, where he graduated in 1812. He volunteered to serve in the War of 1812. After, he studied law and was admitted into the bar in 1816.[251]

His first literary endeavor was published anonymously in a periodical called *Red Book*. Kennedy was part of the Delphian Club, a literary club that was active between 1816 and 1825.[252] While his passion was in literature, he served as a member of the state house of delegates from 1821 to 1823.[253] In 1832, he published *Swallow Barn, or A Sojourn in the Old Dominion*.

In June 1833, the *Baltimore Saturday Visiter* announced a literary contest. Kennedy was one of the judges, and Poe submitted poetry and short stories hoping to win prizes in each category. Poe won the short story portion of the contest but did not win the poetry portion; he believed he had been cheated.[254] The contest did more than give Poe credit for his writing; it introduced him to Kennedy, who would become a counselor, friend and patron willing to help Poe when he was in need. Kennedy would later write, "Our country has produced no poet or prose writer superior to him—indeed, I think, none equal to him."[255]

In 1835, Kennedy's novel *Horse-Shoe Robinson: A Tale of the Tory Ascendency in South Carolina, in 1780* was published. In May 1835, Poe reviewed the work for the *Southern Literary Messenger*. This was partly thanks to Kennedy, who had advised Poe to contact White.[256] The letters between Poe and Kennedy give a deeper meaning to the term *starving artist*. Poe could not accept Kennedy's dinner invitations because he did not have the proper attire and asked Kennedy to loan him twenty dollars.[257] A later entry in Kennedy's diary offers the details in which he helped Poe. Kennedy wrote, "I found him in Baltimore in a state of starvation. I gave him clothing, free access to my table and the use of a horse for exercise whenever he chose; in fact I brought him up from the very verge of despair."[258] Poe continued asking Kennedy for financial support for the remainder of his life, and Kennedy continually gave him advice as well as money when he could.

Kennedy served in Congress from 1838 to 1839 and again from 1841 to 1845 as part of the Whig Party.[259] He continued being involved in literary affairs and being a supportive friend to Poe, acknowledging his success in his career. At the end of 1845, Kennedy wrote to Poe, "I hear of you very often, and although I perceive you have some enemies, it may gratify you to know that you have also a good array of friends."[260]

After Poe's death, Kennedy served as secretary of the navy in the cabinet of President Fillmore from July 22, 1852, to March 7, 1853.[261]

Kennedy died on August 18, 1870, while visiting Newport, Rhode Island. He is buried in Green Mount Cemetery.[262] In his will, he gave his personal archives to the Peabody Institute in Baltimore with the instructions that his papers should be "sealed in a walnut box and kept at the Peabody unopened until 1900 when they become the property of the Institute and available for use by others."[263]

THE GRAVE

Kennedy's grave is a die, base and cap. His epitaph reads, "In Memory of John Pendleton Kennedy, born in Baltimore October 25th, 1795, died in Newport August 18th, 1870." On one side of his marker, the inscription reads, "Author. Statesman. Patriot. He adorned every path which He pursued: and after a prosperous and happy life died in all the blessedness of the Christian's hope." The other side of the marker reads, "Graduated at Baltimore College 1812, admitted to Baltimore Bar 1816, Delegate in Maryland Legislative 1820, Representative in Congress 1838, Speaker of the House of Delegates of Maryland, 1846. Secretary of the Navy, 1852, Provost of the University of Maryland 1850, President of the Peabody Institute 1860." The back of his marker reads, "Blessed are the pure in heart for they shall see God. Matthew 5:8."

GRAVE REFLECTIONS

I met Kennedy on my second visit to the cemetery. I had noticed his wife's memorial on my first visit, as it is a statue of a young girl and a dog. The girl's head is hanging downward while the dog is looking up at her with its paw on her thigh. The girl's left hand rests beside that paw, and a flower stem is on her lap. There is a rose near her crossed feet. The dog's left front paw is standing on top of a snake whose tongue is sticking out next to the girl's right foot. The memorial is quite detailed, and Kennedy's is somewhat plain in comparison. Another aspect of Kennedy's grave is the juxtaposition of the modern city buildings beyond the cemetery. When looking at Kennedy's grave from one angle, there is cemetery-scape behind it; rotating one's angle slightly puts the city as the backdrop.

Left: The grave of John Pendleton Kennedy. *Author's collection.*

Below: The graves of John Pendleton Kennedy and Elizabeth Gray Kennedy. *Author's collection.*

18

Philip Pendleton Cooke

(1816–1850)

Burwell Cemetery, Millwood, Virginia
Facing Route 255 near the southern wall
Southern poet and literary colleague

I do not think that any one so well enters into the poetical portion of my mind as yourself—and I deduce this idea from my intense appreciation of those points of your own poetry which seem lost upon others.[264]
—Poe

Cooke took his time writing eloquent letters to those in the literary world. He greatly admired Poe's work and appreciated all that gentleman did to secure his own success. Could he make the time to compose with all his earthly obligations? First, he had to respond to this letter.

LIFE BEFORE THE STONE

Philip Pendleton Cooke was born on October 26, 1816, to John Rogers Cooke and Maria *Pendleton* Cooke in Martinsburg, Virginia, which is now part of West Virginia. When Cooke was just a boy, his family moved to Winchester, Virginia. In 1831, he enrolled in the College of New Jersey, which would become Princeton University.[265]

Under the pseudonym Larry Lyle, Cooke contributed poems to *The Knickerbocker; or New York Monthly Magazine*.[266] He graduated in 1834 and returned to Winchester, where he studied law. In 1837, Cooke married Willianne Corbin Tayloe Burwell, who had been adopted by her uncle after her father's death. The uncle disapproved of their marriage but still built them a home called the Vineyard in Clarke County.[267] The couple would have five children.

In 1835, Poe was writing for the *Southern Literary Messenger*. The paper's owner, Thomas W. White, had written to Cooke's father asking him to contribute to the magazine. Instead, he passed the request to his son. P.P. Cooke published his poem "Young Rosalie Lee" in the same issue as Poe's "Berenice."[268] Rufus Wilmot Griswold, who would later write Poe's obituary that was intended to hurt the poet's reputation, called Cooke the best poet in Virginia.[269]

Poe and Cooke became friends through letters commenting on and praising each other's work to one another and to their friends. In a letter to Nathaniel Beverly Tucker, a William & Mary College professor whose judgment Poe greatly respected, Poe wrote, "I have met with no one, with the exception of yourself & P.P. Cooke of Winchester, whose judgment concerning these Tales I place any value upon. Generally, people praise extravagantly those of which I am ashamed, and pass in silence what I fancy to be praise worthy."[270] Poe sought advice and feedback from Cooke, and Cooke gave it, not always simply praising Poe's work but noting how he could improve his stories. Nevertheless, Cooke admired Poe's work. He wrote:

I have always found some one remarkable thing in your stories to haunt me long after reading them. The teeth in Berenice—the changing eyes of Morella—that red & glaring crack in the House of Usher—the pores of the deck in the MS. found in a Bottle—the visible drops falling into the goblet in Ligeia, &c. &c.—there is always something of this sort to stick by the mind—by mine at least.[271]

Burwell Cemetery gate. *Author's collection.*

In 1840, Cooke's most famous poem, "Florence Vane," was published in *Burton's Gentleman's Magazine* while Poe was editor. In 1843, he published "Life in the Autumn Woods" and "The Power of the Bards" in the *Southern Literary Messenger.*[272]

In 1847, Griswold and John Pendleton Kennedy, who was Cooke's cousin and also the one who encouraged Poe to reach out to White so that he could submit pieces to the *Messenger,* helped Cooke publish his collection of poems *Froissart Ballads: And Other Poems.*[273]

In 1848, Cooke tried his hand at prose, publishing "John Carper, The Hunter of Lost River" and the next year "The Crime of Andrew Blair" in the *Southern Literary Messenger.*[274]

After Poe's death in 1849, Cooke wrote to John R. Thompson, who took over the *Southern Literary Messenger* after White's death: "Poor Poe will be greatly missed." He noted, "How the world is ringing now with the name and fame of poor Poe, whom the same world starved and 'maddened to drink and destruction.'"[275] In the same letter, Cooke shared, "Poe has always backed me with his praise, and I owe what little repute I possess as yet in the North, more to him than to any other ten men."[276]

The grave of Philip Pendleton Cooke. *Author's collection.*

On January 20, 1850, Cooke contracted pneumonia after wading in icy water during a duck hunting expedition. He is buried in Burwell Cemetery in Millwood, Virginia.

The Grave

Philip Pendleton Cooke's grave is by his wife and some of his children. His marker is an ornate die in socket with a lyre in the center. The stone is cut in a way that mimics the curves of the instrument. The epitaph reads, "Philip Pendleton Cooke died January 20, 1850 Aged 33 years, 2 months and 25 days."

Grave Reflections

Visiting Philip Pendleton Cooke at Burwell Cemetery was one of the most magical stops on my journey. The town of Millwood enchanted me with its winding country roads lined by stone walls. The huge cemetery trees shaded many of the graves. It was a sunny spring day in the low eighties, and the dappled sunlight added to a picturesque setting. I could not imagine a more beautiful cemetery for such a poet. Although summer had not gone and October was not near, the setting evoked Cooke's poem "Life in the Autumn Woods." I read it, as it seemed fitting. Cooke's gravestone suits his personality, which comes through in his letters and poetry. He seemed like someone who would appreciate a gorgeous gravestone, and I'm glad he has one and that it's in mostly good shape.

19

Amasa Converse

(1795–1872)

Cave Hill Cemetery, Louisville, Kentucky
Section P Lot: 424 Grave: 2
Presbyterian minister, publisher
and the man who married Poe and Virginia

*I can afford to wait a century for readers when God himself
has waited six thousand years for an observer.*[277]
—*Poe*

Amasa Converse had a strong belief in the word of God; he was also a man of words, publishing Presbyterian papers throughout his life. While he did not preach to a congregation, he did officiate marriages. Converse noticed his friend's young bride. Was she old enough to marry?

LIFE BEFORE THE STONE

Amasa Converse was born in Lyme, New Hampshire, on August 21, 1795, to Joel Converse and Elizabeth *Bixby* Converse. He was raised in a religious household that worked the land. From a young age, Converse loved learning and would wake early in the morning to complete his household chores before heading off to school. He aspired to see a college and never imagined that he would one day be able to be a college student.[278] In order to earn money for college and desperately wanting to become a scholar, Converse first worked to become a schoolteacher. He attended Smith's Latin Grammar with a private teacher. He then attended Kimball Academy. From there, he set out to Dartmouth College in 1818.[279] He then attended Phillips' Academy.[280] Converse went to Princeton to study theology.[281]

In February 1827, Converse, believing he would be more beneficial as an editor than a preacher, took on the *Family Visitor* and the *Literary and Evangelical Magazine*. Unfortunately, many of the subscribers to the magazines were delinquent in their payments and Converse felt he could not continue in the position.[282]

Later in 1827, Converse became editor of the *Visitor and Telegraph* in Richmond. He would later establish the *Christian Observer* when he combined the *Visitor and Telegraph* with the *Philadelphia Observer*.[283]

On December 16, 1828, Converse married Flavia Booth from Brunswick, Virginia. With her support, Converse was energized and obtained more subscribers to his paper within the next three years, reaching more than three thousand readers.[284] The couple started their family together. In 1831, when visiting New England, they brought home their young niece, who would live with them.[285] The next year, their first child was born.

Nearly a decade after Converse's nuptials, on May 16, 1836, Converse performed the marriage ceremony for his friend Poe to his thirteen-year-old cousin, Virginia Eliza Clemm. The marriage was held in Richmond either at Amasa Converse's home or at Mrs. Yarrington's boardinghouse, where the reception took place.[286] *Southern Literacy Messenger* owner Thomas Willis White and his daughter, Eliza White, were in attendance. Mrs. Yarrington, the boardinghouse owner, and Maria Clemm made the wedding cake.[287] Converse remarked that the bride "looked very young."[288]

In 1838, with controversy within the Presbyterian Church, Converse took over the *Philadelphia Observer* and merged the papers. By January 1839, he had shipped his furniture and printing press and moved to the city. With the merging of the papers, his readership and subscriber list increased.[289]

Converse's sympathies for the South leading up to the Civil War were seen as problematic and even angered locals. On July 5, 1854, his publication office was set on fire and destroyed. All seemed lost until he learned of a friend who saw the office on fire and thought to "burst open the door" and find his books with his subscriber list.[290] When Lincoln was elected in 1860, Converse became outspoken about seceding from the Union. On August 22, 1861, he was arrested, with his newspaper being suspended and his personal property confiscated.[291] When Converse was released, he was able to move the paper to Richmond, where he wrote, preached and visited prisons and hospitals. When Richmond was burned in April 1865, Converse's office escaped the fate of so many buildings surrounding it.[292] Having lost so much already, Converse again moved the paper in 1869. The *Christian Observer* merged with the *Free Christian Commonwealth* and became the *Christian Observer and Commonwealth* out of Louisville.[293]

Three of Converse's children became ordained ministers; his sons assisted him with the newspaper.[294] On December 9, 1872, after a short illness, Amasa Converse passed away at home.[295]

THE GRAVE

Amasa Converse shares a large die on base gravestone with his wife, Flavia Booth. The epitaph reads, "A. Converse, D.D. / 1795–1872 / The Lord is My Shepherd / I Shall Not Want /— Flavia Booth / Wife of A. Converse, D.D. / 1804–1885 / Not of the World / Even As I am Not / Of the World."

GRAVE REFLECTIONS

This was my first visit to Cave Hill Cemetery. After driving 559 miles from my home outside of Richmond, Virginia, I arrived at the cemetery twenty minutes before it closed for the day. This was just enough time for me to drive through and find the grave of Amasa Converse. The gravestone was much larger than I imagined; as it was in a prominent location, I visited Reverend Converse's grave nearly a dozen times over the next few days as I vacationed with the dead. Using the cemetery's tour app, I took myself on a tour of the "Notable Women of Cave Hill Cemetery," and I visited the graves of numerous writers, poets and intellectuals, including Mary Cummings Paine Eudy (1874–1952), fashion designer and poet;

The grave of Amasa Converse. *Author's collection.*

Cave Hill Cemetery chapel. *Author's collection.*

Alice Hegan Rice (1870–1942), author of the best-selling *Mrs. Wiggs of the Cabbage Patch* (1901); and George Keats (1797–1841), the younger brother of Romantic poet John Keats. With 296 acres, I had much to see. It was also molting season for Canada geese, and the Kentucky Department of Fish and Wildlife Resources was banding each goose to help with monitoring the effects of the goose population.

20

Maria Poe Clemm

(1790–1871)

Westminster Burying Ground, Baltimore, Maryland
Near front gate facing Fayette Street
Mother, caregiver, Poe's aunt and mother-in-law

*Maria attending her during her long & tedious illness with a Christian and
martyr-like fortitude, and with a constancy of attention, and unremitting
affection, which must exalt her character in the eyes of all who know her. Maria
is now the only survivor of my grandfather's family.*[296]
—*Poe*

Some of Poe's friends thought she was "like a cat" and could be
untrustworthy and "cruel,"[297] but Muddy cared for the poet like her own
son and he adored her for it. Did she do what she needed to survive? Always.
Even if it meant begging.

LIFE BEFORE THE STONE

Maria Poe was born on March 17, 1790, as the sixth child to Elizabeth *Cairnes* Poe and General David Poe. Her older brother David Poe Jr. was born in 1784, and her sister Elizabeth was born in 1792. The family lived in Baltimore.[298]

By 1805, her brother had quit law school to become an actor and soon found himself married with three children. A Poe family tradition included sending the grandchildren to stay with David and Elizabeth.[299] Maria may have known them, including her nephew Edgar Poe, when they were children coming to visit their grandparents. Maria's brother disappeared, and then his wife, Eliza Poe, died in December 1811, leaving the children orphans. The oldest, Henry, came to stay with the Poe family in Baltimore. Edgar and Rosalie would stay with wealthy Richmond families.

In September 1814, Maria Poe's father joined the Maryland Militia during the Battle of North Point. General Poe died two years later.[300] Within a year, in July 1817, when she was twenty-seven years old, Maria married a hardware merchant, William Clemm Jr. Her husband had been married to her cousin, Harriet Poe. He entered the marriage with five children from his first marriage.[301] Together, the couple would have three children including Henry Clemm, Virginia Marie Clemm, who died when she was just two years old, and Virginia Eliza Clemm who would later become the wife of Edgar Allan Poe.

In 1826, William Clemm passed away, leaving Maria Clemm to care for two young children. Her husband left them little after his passing, and because relatives had opposed the marriage, Maria found herself desperate to make ends meet.[302] Her sewing helped support the family. She also took in boarders. Like her brother had done before and her nephew would do, Maria begged for money.[303] Fortunately, the annual pension her mother received that was on behalf of Maria's father's military involvement helped to support the entire family.[304]

By 1832, Edgar Poe had been discharged from the army, argued with his foster father, John Allan, and moved to Baltimore to live with the Poe family, including his grandmother, aunt and cousins. The next few years were exceptionally challenging for Maria. Her mother passed away in 1835, which also ended the pension the family relied on. Her son, Henry, died, leaving Virginia Eliza Clemm her only surviving child.[305] Her nephew Edgar Poe had also left the family to head to Richmond, where he would work as the editor of the *Southern Literary Messenger* after having his short stories published in the paper. With a great deal of uncertainty about her and her daughter's fates, Josephine *Clemm* Poe, half sister to Virginia, and her husband, Neilson Poe, offered to take in Virginia and Maria Clemm. The offer promised housing security and an education for Virginia.[306] Maria wrote to Edgar Poe explaining the proposition, "simply a plan…to bring matters to the satisfactory conclusion which she desired," as she had "a strong and determined will" and was easily able to persuade her nephew.[307] Edgar Poe felt insulted by the offer, believing Neilson Poe was trying to break up what semblance of family he had. Edgar Poe wrote to his aunt, "The tone of your letter wounds me to the soul—Oh Aunty, aunty you loved me once—how can you be so cruel now? You speak of Virginia acquiring accomplishments, and entering into society—you speak in so worldly a tone. Are you sure she would be more happy."[308] His words must have touched her heart, for on May 16, 1836, Poe's status changed from nephew to son-in-law as he married his thirteen-year-old cousin, Virginia Eliza Clemm. Maria Clemm and Mrs. Yarrington, the boardinghouse owner, made the wedding cake.[309]

Edgar and Virginia *Clemm* Poe, along with Maria Clemm, moved to New York in 1837 and then to Philadelphia in 1838, where Poe would begin writing short stories. Poe's writing was gaining attention. He was productive and happy, and he finally had the stable family life for which he longed. Maria also had her own stable life as the matriarch of the family. Poe called her "Muddy" and treated her as he would his own mother. Sadly, this happiness was brief. In January 1842, Virginia burst a blood vessel and began showing signs of tuberculosis. Poe and Maria focused on Virginia's health. In one letter, Poe details Virginia's wellness and happiness. He refers to Virginia as "Sis" or "Sissy," writing, "Sis is delighted, and we are both in excellent spirits. She has coughed hardly any and had no night sweat."[310] With Virginia's health deteriorating, the family moved to New York in April 1844, where Poe would work for the *Sunday Times*. The family moved again in May 1846 to a small cottage in Fordham, New York. While there were moments when Virginia's health seemed to improve, a notice in the paper shares that Virginia and Edgar Poe were "dangerously ill" in January 1847.[311] Virginia must have known that she would not live long. She begged her mother, "Muddy, will you console and take care of my poor Eddy—you will never never leave him? Promise me, my dear Muddy, and then I can die in peace."[312] Virginia died on January 30, 1847. Maria kept her promise to her daughter and did not leave Poe. She supported him emotionally through many trials, including his engagement to Sarah H. Whitman in December 1848.[313] When Poe was traveling on his book tour during the summer of

1849, he wrote to Maria, "I am so homesick....I never wanted to see any one half so bad as I want to see my own darling mother. It seems to me that I would make any sacrifice to hold you by the hand once more, and get you to cheer me up, for I am terribly depressed."[314] In July 1849, Poe wrote again sharing that he was sick and how much he missed her: "I love you better than ten thousand lives—so much so that it is cruel in you to let me leave you; nothing but sorrow ever comes of it."[315] Within a week, Poe was rejuvenated and regained his spirits. He wrote, "All is not lost yet, and 'the darkest hour is just before daylight.' Keep up heart, my own beloved mother—all may yet go well. I will put forth all my energies. When I get my mind a little more composed, I will try to write something."[316]

Poe's poem "To My Mother" was published on July 7, 1849. The poem's focus is clearly on his relationship with his mother-in-law. In Poe's August 1849 letter to Maria, he wrote of Elmira *Royster* Shelton and their impending marriage; he planned to bring Maria to live with the reunited love from his youth.[317] He reemphasized his plan in his September 10, 1849 letter to Maria from Old Point Comfort, Virginia. Poe's final letter to his mother-in-law was on September 18, 1849. Again, Poe wrote of his engagement: "Elmira has just got home from the country. I spent last evening with her. I think she loves me more devotedly than any one I ever knew & I cannot help loving her in return."[318] He added, "I hope that our troubles are nearly over."[319]

After Poe died in Baltimore on October 7, 1849, Maria's troubles worsened. Without any source of income or family members to turn to, she reached out to Poe's friends and admirers, including Henry W. Longfellow and Charles Dickens, to receive support.[320] For the next decade, Maria did not have a stable home life. She went to Brooklyn, New York, and then on to Lowell, Massachusetts; Milford, Connecticut; Alexandria, Virginia; Putnam, Ohio; and Baltimore, Maryland. She stayed with Poe's friends and admirers, including Sarah H. Whitman and Annie Locke Richmond.[321]

She had given Rufus Griswold a power of attorney, which enabled him to publish an edition of Poe's prose and poetry with the assurance that after publishing costs Maria would receive profits from the sales. This did not come to fruition.[322] Griswold wrote a scathing obituary that deliberately perpetuated rumors about Poe, including that he had been expelled from the University of Virginia, had abandoned his army duties and even tried to seduce John Allan's second wife.[323] While Poe's friends would try to set the record straight, the damage had been done, and many of these misrepresentations are still shared today.

The grave of Maria Poe Clemm. *Author's collection.*

Maria Clemm also disagreed with Poe's sister, Rosalie, who believed she was the heir to her brother's possessions.[324] Both of the women would struggle financially in their later years.

In 1863, after moving several times, Maria hoped to be admitted to the Baltimore Widow's Home but was unable to secure the entrance fee. Instead, she became a resident of the Episcopal Church Home, which was then located in the same building where Poe died. Maria died on February 16, 1871.[325] She had outlived her husband, children and son-in-law. Maria Clemm's death was announced in the paper: "At her own request she was buried by the side of her 'darling Eddie' in Westminster Churchyard.... There were about a dozen ladies and two gentlemen present, admirers of Poe and friends of Mrs. Clemm. Among the ladies in attendance was Rosalie Poe."[326]

THE GRAVE

In 1875, when a monument was dedicated to Poe in a prominent part of the churchyard, Maria Clemm's remains were relocated to the new plot to rest beside Poe.[327] Edgar Allan Poe's monument is a die, base and cap. The cap features decorative elements including a lyre and foliage above the base symbolizing the connection between heaven and earth. On the base of the marker there are floral accents above each epitaph. Her name was added to the monument in 1977.[328] Maria Clemm's epitaph faces the street and can be seen even when the churchyard is closed. It reads, "Maria Poe Clemm / Born / March 17, 1790 / Died / February 18, 1871."

GRAVE REFLECTIONS

Reflecting on someone independently from those with whom she shares a monument is nearly impossible, but I think Maria Clemm would like that her memory is still attached to her Eddie. Maria once had numerous letters from him, but she was too generous with each request from Poe's admirers, and in the end, she gave them away and was left with a simple autograph. She believed that the dead lived on in our memories, writing to Annie Richmond, "Oh memory, memory, how faithful it *still* is."[329]

21

Virginia Eliza Clemm Poe

(1822–1847)

Westminster Burying Ground, Baltimore, Maryland
Near front gate on Fayette Street
Poe's cousin and wife

I should have lost my courage but for you—my little darling wife you are my greatest and only stimulus now, to battle with this uncongenial, unsatisfactory and ungrateful life.[330]
—*Poe*

Sissy was a pale, young beauty who captured her cousin's heart and became a child bride who would be immortalized in writing. Would the fresh air restore her health? Her husband wrote, "The death, then, of a beautiful woman is, unquestionably, the most poetical topic in the world."[331]

LIFE BEFORE THE STONE

Virginia Eliza Clemm was born on August 15, 1822, in Baltimore, Maryland, to Maria *Poe* Clemm and William Clemm. She was the youngest of five half siblings and one older brother, Henry, and she was named after a sister who had died just two years before her birth. Her father was a merchant until his death in 1826, which left the family with little provisions.[332] Her mother's sewing helped support the family.[333] Her grandmother's annual pension from her grandfather's military involvement was the family's main source of income.[334]

By 1832, Virginia's first cousin Edgar Poe had left the army and moved to Baltimore to live with them. Those years were challenging for the family, as her grandmother passed away, ending the annual financial support, and her brother died.[335] Her cousin Edgar A. Poe had also gone to Richmond to work for the *Southern Literary Messenger*. Noticing the family's situation, half sister Josephine *Clemm* Poe and her husband, Neilson Poe, offered to take in Virginia and her mother, offering shelter and even an education for the young girl.[336] Edgar Poe was so hurt by the proposal that he wrote his aunt and proposed marriage to Virginia within that letter. Poe wrote, "Virginia! do not go!—do not go where you can be comfortable & perhaps happy—and on the other hand can I calmly resign my—life itself.…My love, my own sweetest Sissy, my darling little wifey, think well before you break the heart of your Cousin, Eddy."[337] The letter insinuates that there had been some discussion of marriage prior. At the time of the letter, Virginia had just turned thirteen. Virginia's agency to accept a proposal of marriage as a poor, young girl is debated among scholars. Girls marrying young was somewhat normalized at this point in American history. The U.S. Census Bureau did not connect age and marital status until 1880, at which time 11.7 percent of fifteen- to nineteen-year-old girls were wives.[338] Not quite a month after Poe's letter to his aunt, he obtained a marriage license on September 22, 1835.[339] On May 16, 1836, Virginia married her twenty-seven-year-old cousin, although some speculate there may have been a secret marriage that took place prior to the public Richmond wedding.[340] Although girls married at Virginia's age, her age was listed as twenty-one.[341] The minister, Reverend Amasa Converse, believed Virginia "looked very young."[342] After the wedding, the couple traveled to Petersburg for their honeymoon, staying with Hiram Haines and his wife, Mary Ann *Philpotts* Haines.[343]

Within a year, Edgar and Virginia *Clemm* Poe, along with her mother, moved to New York and then to Philadelphia in 1838, where Poe's writing gained recognition. Her husband was productive and happy and even had the opportunity to meet Charles Dickens, whose pet raven Grip amused Poe so much that he described him in his review of Dickens's *Barnaby Rudge* (1841). Many Poe scholars believe the pet was the inspiration for Poe's poem "The Raven" (1845).[344] Virginia began showing signs of tuberculosis by the time she was twenty-one.[345] Poe was a doting husband as his wife was frequently confined to her bed.[346]

With Virginia's health deteriorating, the family moved to New York; 1845 was considered Poe's *annus mirabilis*, or his miraculous year. In January, "The Raven" was published in the *Evening Mirror*. The publication made Poe popular at literary salons. In March, poet Frances Osgood asked to be introduced to Poe, as he had favorably reviewed her poetry. After their meeting—and regardless of both poets being married—each published flirtatious poems to the other in the *Broadway Journal*. Knowing of the relationship, Virginia invited Osgood over and encouraged their correspondence, believing that Osgood had a "restraining" effect on her husband.[347] Poe also received attention from another poet, Elizabeth Ellet. To obscure her flirtations in her letters, she wrote portions in German,

Charles Mills Sheldon, artist, *Poe at Work. Illustration from* Cassell's Book of Knowledge *(circa 1910) (London: The Waverley Book Company, Ltd.) lithograph.*

although it appears that Poe was unable to understand what she had written.[348] Jealousy ensued, and Poe believed Ellet acted maliciously toward him by trying to involve Virginia in private letters he exchanged with Osgood.[349] In February 1846, he sent Osgood a Valentine's Day poem, while Virginia sent him one that included an acrostic poem with the first letter of each line spelling her husband's name.[350]

Within a few months of the scandal, in May 1846, the family moved to Fordham, New York, in hopes of restoring Virginia's health. This was the retreat Virginia had longed for, with her husband rarely leaving the cottage, writing and tending to their garden. In a later letter, Poe shared, "She recovered partially and I again hoped. At the end of a year...I went through precisely the same scene…then again—again—again & even once again at varying intervals. Each time I felt all the agonies of her death."[351] With Virginia's health not improving, there were rumors that Poe had become insane. Poe wrote, "I loved her more dearly & clung to her life with more desperate pertinacity. But I am constitutionally sensitive—nervous in a very unusual degree. I became insane, with long intervals of horrible sanity."[352] When Poe left for work, everyone in the household was affected, including Catterina, their pet cat, who refused to eat while Poe was gone.[353]

A newspaper reported that Virginia and her husband were "dangerously ill" in January 1847.[354] Virginia died on January 30, 1847. Poe commissioned a portrait of his wife before her burial.[355] Virginia was buried in the Valentine family vault in the nearby Dutch Reformed Church graveyard.[356] Like he had for many other significant women in his life, Poe visited Virginia's grave frequently.

The Grave

Virginia Poe was originally buried in the Dutch Reformed Cemetery churchyard in a family vault belonging to their Fordham landlords. In 1875, after a campaign for a proper monument to the author, Poe was reinterred in a prominent part of Westminster Burying Ground and Maria Clemm's remains were relocated to the new lot to rest beside Poe.[357] Virginia Poe was not reinterred immediately. A decade after, she was reinterred on January 19, 1885. The monument she shares with her husband and mother is a die, base and cap with decorative elements including a lyre and foliage above the base. Her name was added to the monument in 1977.[358] Virginia *Clemm* Poe's epitaph reads, "Virginia Clemm Poe / Born / August 15, 1822 / Died / January 30, 1847."

Grave Reflections

Once hearing the story of Virginia's reinterment to Westminster Burying Ground, it is hard not to think about her bones being stashed in a small box and being stored under Poe biographer William F. Gill's bed for two years. As the story was told, Gill happened to be visiting the cemetery as part was being razed and exactly when the sexton held Virginia's bones piled on a

The grave of Virginia Clemm Poe. *Author's collection.*

shovel. As Gill shares, the plan was to toss her bones aside since no family was there to claim them. Instead, Gill placed her bones in a small box and took them home with him. He then contacted relatives, including Neilson Poe, to eventually have them reinterred next to her husband. However, while he had the bones, he would bring them out for those who admired Poe's work as a macabre form of show-and-tell.[359]

22

Hiram Haines

(1802–1841)

*We need the assistance of all our friends and
count upon yourself among the foremost.*[360]
—*Poe*

Hiram Haines was a man of many words. The most eloquent were saved for his lovely wife. To readers, he was known only as "The Stranger." Poe and Haines had much in common—poets, editors, newspapermen. Even with a packed house, when his friend married, how could he not offer to host a honeymoon suite?

Life Before the Stone

Hiram Haines was born on November 29, 1802, in Delamore Forest, Culpeper County, Virginia, to Ezekiel Haines and Anna *Hopkins* Haines.[361] He did not receive any formal education but was interested in poetry and family history from a young age. By the 1820s, he had compiled a private notebook that included his own prose and poetry. At this time, he may have also worked as a printer's apprentice or news reporter.[362]

On October 29, 1824, the Marquis de Lafayette visited Petersburg. Haines's poem "Lafayette's Welcome to Petersburg" was recited during the visit, and this solidified the young poet's reputation.[363] The next year,

Haines published a book of poetry, *Mountain Buds and Blossoms, Wove in a Rustic Garland*, signing his work from "The Stranger."[364]

Haines continued to build his reputation as a poet and writer and began to travel to North Carolina and Washington, D.C., for work, where he was a collection agent for merchant houses and tobacco magnates.[365] He contributed to local newspapers during this time. In 1826, he married Mary Ann Currie Philpotts, who had been a childhood friend of Poe in Richmond.[366] Haines wrote his wife detailed letters while traveling in order for them to stay connected.[367] While it must have been challenging to be apart at the start of their marriage, Haines's writing shows that his heart remained with Mary even if he was elsewhere.

By the early 1830s, Haines had begun publishing the *American Constellation*.[368] Along with his business partner, W.H. Davis, they published a newspaper and solicited publications, including books and pamphlets. After 1835, Haines independently published the paper and included his own poetry under the alias "The Stranger." He was admitted to the Petersburg Benevolent Mechanic Association as a printer that same year.[369]

Haines's family was growing and now included four children. They lived in a house in Petersburg that included a storefront property where he established Merchants' Coffee House, which was also known as Hiram Haines' Coffee House.[370] This was a place to come together for food, drink and lively discussions about literature and politics with regular visitors, including "an eclectic blend of intellectuals, journalists, craftsmen, aristocrats, wanders and performers."[371]

After Poe's marriage to his cousin Virginia on May 16, 1836, the couple traveled to Petersburg for their honeymoon. The Poes were already acquainted with the Haineses, and Poe had visited Hiram Haines's wife, Mary Ann *Philpotts* Haines, at least one time prior to this visit.[372] Petersburg was considered a place people traveled to for entertainment, including horse racing, taverns and the theater. Poe's mother had performed in Petersburg during her acting career, and during this time, she must not have been far from Poe's thoughts.

During the couple's honeymoon, Edgar and Virginia Poe visited several homes of other journalists and even a former editor of the *Southern Literary Messenger*, Edwin V. Sparhawk.[373] While Poe's life seemed promising with his role at the newspaper in Richmond, Haines struggled collecting the debts owed to both the *American Constellation* and his coffeehouse. He resorted to putting up his personal assets as collateral. In 1838, because of continued financial struggles, Haines had to surrender the paper.[374]

The next year, in 1839, he started a new paper, *Time O' Day* (also called *Peep O' Day*), without much success, but he would find it the next year with the *Virginia Star*, which he published until January 1841. It was in the *Virginia Star* where Haines promoted Poe's work, and in turn, Poe promoted Haines's paper. Poe saw promise in the paper, writing, "The 'Star' has my very best wishes, and if you really intend to push it with energy, there cannot be a doubt of its full success."[375]

Poe and Haines continued to be close friends and supporters of each other's endeavors. Haines even offered to send Virginia a fawn. Poe had to decline the offer, not knowing how they would transport the animal from Petersburg to Philadelphia, where the Poes were living at that time.[376]

On January 14, 1841, after a brief illness, Hiram Haines passed away at Hickory Hill in Prince George County. He was survived by his wife, six young children and his father. His obituary described him as "a man of taste and talents" and that people "will long remember his inestimable worth—his blameless integrity—his uniform kindness to all, and the characteristic generosity."[377]

THE GRAVE

Hiram Haines is buried in a family plot in Blandford Cemetery in Peterburg, approximately one mile from his former coffeehouse on 12 West Bank Street. The gravestone is broken in two places—from the base and across the center. It now rests on its back. The marker reads, "In memory of Hiram Haines, who departed this life 15 Jan'y 1841 Aged 38 years. O Death the palm is thine," lines from Edward Young's poem "The Complaint. Night III. Narcissa."[378] Each time I have visited the grave of Hiram Haines, there has always been some type of replica of a raven resting on it or nearby.

GRAVE REFLECTIONS

In June 2019, the River City Cemetarians hosted a moonlight walking tour through Blandford Cemetery. While many might consider a nighttime cemetery tour spooky, it is one of the cooler and more pleasant ways to enjoy a cemetery in humid, hot summers. Just make sure to have permission to visit after hours, since most cemeteries restrict such solo visits. With

Above: Family plot including the graves of Hiram Haines and Mary A.C. Haines. *Author's collection.*

Left: The grave of Hiram Haines. *Author's collection.*

flashlights in hand, Martha Atkinson of the Peterburg Preservation Task Force led guests through the cemetery.

Approximately four miles from the cemetery is the locally notorious "tombstone house," which has a connection with another local cemetery in Petersburg. Located at 1736 Youngs Road, the house was built in the 1930s after the superintendent of the Poplar Grove National Cemetery decided to reduce costs by removing the upright grave markers, cutting off the bottoms that had been in the ground and replacing the top portions of the markers by lying them down flat. This helped grounds crew with maintenance, which has been an ongoing battle in many cemeteries. The 2,220 bottom portions of the markers were sold to a gentleman who proceeded to build his dream house out of the materials. A macabre plot twist to Poe fanfiction or upcycling?

23

THOMAS WILLIS WHITE

(1788–1843)

SAINT JOHN'S EPISCOPAL CHURCHYARD, RICHMOND, VIRGINIA
SECTION J, MARKER 60
SOUTHERN LITERARY MESSENGER FOUNDER AND POE'S BOSS

To be appreciated you must be read.
—Poe

Mr. White helped change Mr. Poe's literary career from poet to journal editor and literary reviewer, which in turn helped his magazine grow. White saw great promise in the young writer who had befriended his daughter, but he also had his concerns. When would Poe respect himself enough to avoid drinking?

LIFE BEFORE THE STONE

Thomas Willis White was born on March 28, 1788, to Thomas White and Sarah Davis White in Yorktown, Virginia. His father worked as a tailor, and the family flourished until 1796, when White's father died from yellow fever.[379] His three siblings and White, who was only eight years old, were affected by their father's death. With a challenging start to life, White became a printer's apprentice to William Rind and John Stuart at the *Virginia Federalist* in Richmond. The family moved to Norfolk, where White would work at the *Norfolk Gazette and Publick Ledger*.[380]

He married Margaret Ann Ferguson on December 12, 1809. The couple set out to have their own family, which began in 1811 when their first daughter, Sarah, was born in Boston while the couple was visiting the city.[381] Their son, Thomas Henry White, was born in 1813. Sadly, his life was cut short on October 7, 1832, at the age of nineteen from "the prevailing epidemic."[382] In 1817, the family moved to Richmond, where White would establish a publishing business. The next year, their daughter Euphania was born on New Year's Eve 1818. In 1820, their daughter Elizabeth "Eliza," who would become a devoted friend to Poe, was born in Richmond. In 1823, a second son, William Alexander, was born but died as a baby. Their family was completed on March 23, 1828, with their daughter Clara Harvey. Life was promising for the self-educated White.

In 1833, White celebrated the marriage of his oldest daughter, Sarah, to Peter Bernard, a publisher, author and direct descendant of Pocahontas.[383] The next year, White established the *Southern Literary Messenger* with the intention of the paper being a platform for southern writers of poetry and prose. The masthead of the newspaper read "Devoted to Every Department of Literature and the Fine Arts."

Perhaps thanks to Poe's friend John Pendleton Kennedy, who wrote a letter of recommendation, Poe's first piece in the *Southern Literary Messenger* was in March 1835, titled "Berenice," a Gothic fiction story about a man named Egaeus preparing to marry his cousin, whose health is deteriorating from disease. The narrator becomes obsessed with his cousin's teeth.[384] In the uncensored version of the story, Egaeus visits Berenice's body after she has died. As he is staring at her corpse, he notices that her finger twitches and her lips part in a smile, exposing her teeth and hinting that she, in fact, is not dead. Later that night, he wakes to find himself covered in mud with a small ebony box nearby. He fears opening the box, which when opened includes dental instruments and "white and glistening" teeth.[385] Although

White received complaints from readers about the violence in Poe's story, Poe was hired on as a staff writer in August 1835, and the revised version was not published until 1840. The complaints also did not stop White from publishing "Morella," another Gothic horror by Poe in the April 1835 issue.[386] In a letter from Poe to White, the author admits, "The subject is by far too horrible, and I confess that I hesitated in sending it you....To be appreciated you must be read, and these things are invariably sought after."[387] In the same letter, Poe admitted that writing the horrific story was part of a bet that he "could produce nothing effective on a subject so singular, provided [he] treated it seriously."[388]

Poe published more than Gothic horror for the *Southern Literary Messenger*. He wrote satire ("Lionizing" May 1835), humor ("Epimanes," March 1836) and adventure ("The Unparalleled Adventure of One Hans Pfaall," June 1835). He also published reviews of books and periodicals, which gave him the reputation of being a premier critic. By the end of 1835, White had promoted Poe to editor.[389] This was not without White's concerns over Poe's use of alcohol. In a letter to Poe, White wrote, "You have fine talents, Edgar, —and you ought to have them respected as well as yourself. Learn to respect yourself, and you will very soon find that you are respected. Separate yourself from the bottle, and bottle companions, for ever [*sic*]!"[390]

In 1836, White celebrated the marriage of his daughter Euphania to Nathan Stedman, a comptroller in North Carolina.[391] In 1837, White became a grandfather twice, first in January with Sarah's first child and then again in May with Euphania's first child. That same year, in January, Poe left the *Southern Literary Messenger*. And White's wife, Margaret, died on December 12, 1837.

On a visit to New York in September 1842, White was "struck with paralysis" while "at the supper table of the Astor-House."[392] That same year, the magazine was sold to Benjamin Blake Minor. After returning home, White died on January 19, 1843. He is buried in St. John's Churchyard with his wife and sons.

THE GRAVE

Poe's boss is buried in Section J, Marker 60. The memorial is a die, base and cap with the inscription, "In memory of T W White, late editor and proprietor of the *Southern Literary Messenger*."

The grave of Thomas Willis White. *Author's collection.*

GRAVE REFLECTIONS

Having an interest in cemeteries, I enjoy learning about those interred there, the cemetery's history and the stonemasons who created the markers. The grave of Thomas Willis White is within a few feet of the grave of Mary G. Royster, the mother of Sarah Elmira Royster Shelton, Poe's first and last fiancée. Royster's grave includes the maker's mark for J.W. Davies, a stonemason from Richmond, Virginia, whose storage yard was damaged in 1864. The stonemason's maker's mark acted as a form of advertising, as the stonemason frequently had other occupations. Davies, who is buried with his family in Hollywood Cemetery, spent half a decade making improvements to the chimney cap. After the disaster to his property, he refocused his energy on publishing music.[393] Whenever I see his mark throughout Virginia, I am reminded of my delight when my husband and I visited Montpelier, the home to President James Madison and his wife, Dolley, after our marriage in Orange, Virginia. Dolley Madison's obelisk includes the maker's mark of J.W. Davies. Talk about feeling like a cemetery nerd. Some people get excited when seeing her tiny wedding band; I felt connected to both history and home by seeing Davies's maker's mark.

Eliza White

(1820–1888)

Shockoe Hill Cemetery, Richmond, Virginia
Range 26, Sec. 16, Q.S. 4
Shakespearean reader, daughter of
the *Southern Literary Messenger* owner and Poe's friend

> *Eliza!—let thy generous heart*
> *From its present pathway part not!*[394]
> *—Poe*

Eliza White was literary and lovely. While she was often considered the belle of the ball, who could possibly be lovelier than Mr. Poe's blushing bride?

Life Before the Stone

Elizabeth White was born in 1820 in Richmond to Thomas Willis White and Margaret Ann *Ferguson* White. She was one of five children, including two brothers who both passed—leaving only Eliza and her sisters.[395]

In 1833, her oldest sister, Sarah, married Peter Bernard, a publisher, author and later editor.[396] The following year, her father established the *Southern Literary Messenger* when she was about fourteen years old. She would meet Poe while he was working at her father's paper when she was about fifteen and Poe was twenty-six. Poe became a frequent visitor to the family home, where literature was the focus. Eliza had lovely blonde hair and stunning blue eyes. She was easily considered the belle of the ball.

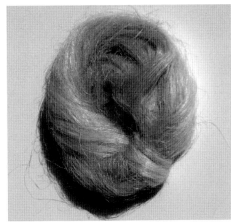

Right: Lock of hair from Eliza White.
Edgar Allan Poe Museum.

Below: Unmarked grave of Eliza White.
Author's collection.

While there may have been early flirtations between the two, they became lifelong friends. Eliza visited Poe at Maria Clemm's home in Philadelphia and visited Poe and his wife in Fordham, New York.[397]

On May 16, 1836, when Poe married his young cousin Virginia Clemm, he was joined by close friends during the wedding ceremony. Eliza and her father were guests.[398]

Eliza became a poet and was "renowned as a Shakespearean reader."[399] She never married. Records show that she died in 1888 and is buried in Shockoe Hill Cemetery. A lock of her hair can be seen at the Poe Museum in Richmond.[400]

THE GRAVE

Eliza is buried in an unmarked grave in the plot belonging to Eliza's sister's daughter Ellen Bernard. Sarah and her family are buried here. None have grave markers.

GRAVE REFLECTIONS

It may seem unusual to include Eliza White in a book that is somewhat focused on grave markers; however, her relationship to Poe and to Richmond history is significant. Because Shockoe Hill Cemetery has kept records of burials, Eliza's grave is easy to find. The Friends of Shockoe Hill Cemetery have been amazing stewards recognizing the importance of this history. They have been able to not only repair broken gravestones but also place more than three hundred individual gravestones and interpretative markers. It is not out of the question to believe that Eliza and her family's graves might one day be marked.

25

Elizabeth Van Lew

(1818–1900)

SHOCKOE HILL CEMETERY, RICHMOND, VIRGINIA
RANGE 8, SEC. 5, Q.S. 4
ABOLITIONIST AND SPY; POE READ "THE RAVEN"
IN HER FAMILY PARLOR AND DISCUSSED MESMERISM

The customs of the world are so many conventional follies.[401]
—*Poe*

Elizabeth Van Lew's parlor was the perfect place for Poe to read his poetry and discuss recent scientific discoveries. Years later, she watched the famous author visit his childhood sweetheart, who lived down the street.

Those summer evenings conjured so much romance for some women, but others knew storms were brewing in the country. How could a Southern "lady" ever be suspected of such crimes?

LIFE BEFORE THE STONE

Elizabeth Van Lew was born on October 15, 1818, in Richmond to John Van Lew and Eliza *Baker* Van Lew. She was the eldest daughter. Her sister, Anna Pauline, was born in 1820; her brother, John Newton, was born in 1823. The family lived in a mansion on Church Hill. Aside from being educated in Philadelphia, Van Lew resided in her childhood home throughout her lifetime.

Her father was one of the leading hardware merchants of Richmond, and the family lived in luxury. Her family was part of Richmond Society and lived on Twenty-Third and Grace Streets on Church Hill, where "Edgar Allan Poe had read 'The Raven' aloud in its spacious parlor."[402]

According to family tradition, Poe also "conducted static electricity experiments" and discussed "mesmeristic science."[403] Mesmerism, protoscientific theory coined by German doctor Granz Mesmer, was a natural force possessed by all living things from humans to animals. Poe's short story "The Facts in the Case of M. Valdemar" was based on the idea that a person could be entranced at the very moment of death and be in a suspended state until removed from the trance. Many readers at the time believed the fictional story was instead a scientific report, including Robert Hanham Collyer, a mesmerist and phrenologist. On December 16, 1845, Collyer wrote Poe asking if his story was "merely a splendid creation of your own brain, not having any truth in fact."[404] Collyer must have been disappointed to learn the truth. In 1847, Poe admitted, "'The Valdemar Case' was a hoax, of course."[405]

Later in life, Elizabeth Van Lew remembered seeing Poe visiting Elmira *Royster* Shelton on summer evenings during their courtship in 1849. Van Lew lived a half block from Shelton.[406]

After Poe's death, Van Lew, who held strong antislavery views, became a spy for the Union using an underground network and working with coded messages and invisible ink. She even used a codename—Babcock.[407] After the war, she continued living on Church Hill, where locals shunned her for her involvement as a spy. In her obituary, it reads that even St. John's Church, where she had been a member, "closed [their doors] upon her."[408]

The grave of Elizabeth Van Lew. *Author's collection.*

Elizabeth Van Lew died on September 25, 1900. She is buried in Shockoe Hill Cemetery. Her obituary reads, "Miss Van Lew died friendless and alone." Yet it was a group of friends from Massachusetts, including the family of a soldier she had assisted in a jail during the war, who paid for her funeral.[409]

THE GRAVE

Van Lew's grave includes a boulder with a bronze plaque that includes her name and birth and death years. The marker is "from the Capitol Hill in Boston" as a "tribute from Massachusetts friends." The epitaph reads: "She risked everything that was dear to her—friends, fortune, comfort, health, even life itself—all for one absorbing desire of her heart—that slavery might be abolished and the Union preserved."

GRAVE REFLECTIONS

Elizabeth Van Lew is buried in a shady area off the path where the terrain is uneven. There is a sign that points to her grave from the closest road, and considering the size and shape of her marker, it is somewhat easy to find. She was called "Crazy Bet" by Richmonders, and local children thought of her as a witch. Van Lew never married, and I imagine an independent woman with a mind of her own in 1900 was an unusual sight. Some must have found those qualities scary. Some even believed that her mansion was haunted after her death, although the City of Richmond demolished the family home, a decision possibly made in spite of her prior actions. She is said to have helped over one hundred Union prisoners escape Libby Prison.[410] While I cannot recall the first time I visited her grave, I have more than once wondered how someone like Van Lew had the grit to stand up to an entire city who thought she had done them wrong and why my Virginia public education failed to introduce me to her in my youth.

26

WILLIAM GILMORE SIMMS

(1806–1870)

MAGNOLIA CEMETERY, CHARLESTON, SOUTH CAROLINA
LOT 968 OLD
NOVELIST AND POET WHOM POE CALLED
THE BEST WRITER IN AMERICA

The best novelist which this country has, upon the whole, produced.[411]
—*Poe*

His work was the quintessence of southern letters. Could he set aside his region's political concerns to focus on his writing? The war would ruin him.

Life Before the Stone

William Gilmore Simms was born on April 17, 1806, to William Gilmore Simms and his wife, Harriet Ann Augusta *Singleton* Simms. As a young boy, he lost his mother at age two. After the loss of his two older brothers, his father headed to Mississippi, and Simms was raised by his maternal grandmother, who sent him to grammar school taught by the faculty of the College of Charleston.[412] By the time he was twelve, he had studied *materia medica* (the Latin term for medical material) and became a druggist's apprentice.[413] Simms traveled to Mississippi to see his father. When he returned, he studied law and established *The Album*, a literary weekly that would run for a year.[414]

In 1826, Simms married Anna Malcom Giles, and he was admitted to the South Carolina bar.[415] He managed his homelife and work as well as his literary interests. Simms spoke at Fort Moultrie on June 28, 1828, where the enlisted private Edgar A. Perry was stationed.[416] Perry, which was Poe's alias, listened to Simms's oration and may have met him at this time. The prior year, Simms had published two books of Romantic poetry: *Lyrical and Other Poems* (1827) and *Early Lays* (1827). Simms gave readings in Charleston at local bookstores, and it is possible that while on leave, Poe attended one of these readings.[417]

In 1829, Simms purchased the *City Gazette*. While life seemed promising, his father and the grandmother who raised him passed away. He experienced more tragedy when his wife died leaving him with a young daughter.[418] Simms focused his energy on writing and published *The Vision of Cortes, Cain, and Other Poems* (1829); *The Tricolor, or Three Days of Blood in Paris* (1830); *Atalantis, a Tale of the Sea* (1832); the short novel *Martin Faber, the Story of a Criminal* (1833) and *Guy Rivers: A Tale of Georgia* (1834), which earned him decent royalties and allowed him to have a career in writing.

In 1836, he proposed to Chevillette Eliza Roach. The couple would have fourteen children, with only nine living into adulthood.[419] At this time, Simms diversified his writing to include history and biography.

Simms was included in Poe's 1841 "Chapter on Autography," printed in *Graham's Magazine*. Poe analyzed the handwriting of literary figures of the time to determine their personality traits but included more literary criticism than actual handwriting analysis. For Simms, Poe wrote, "As a poet, indeed, we like him far better than as a novelist....Mr. S. has more slope, and more uniformity in detail, with less in the mass—while it has also less of the picturesque, although still much."[420]

By the mid-1840s, Poe had an antagonistic relationship with writers in the North as he further aligned himself as a southern writer. His negative reviews targeted New York writers, who produced counterattacks on his character. In a letter, W. Gilmore Simms encouraged Poe to be cautious with such quarrels:

> *Suffer me to tell you frankly, taking the privilege of a true friend, that you are now perhaps in the most perilous period of your career—just in that position just at that time of life—when a false step becomes a capital error—when a single leading mistake is fatal in its consequences....You must subdue your impulses....I need not say to you that, to a Southern man, the annoyance of being mixed up in a squabble with persons whom he does not know, and does not care to know.*[421]

Simms continued being a prolific writer after Poe's death until the Civil War, which consumed his time and energy. He wrote, "Literature, especially poetry, is effectually overwhelmed by the drums, & the cavalry, and the shouting."[422] His defense of slavery and the South has been criticized. His writing ended soon after the war with his last published works being *A City Laid Waste: The Capture, Sack, and Destruction of the City of Columbia* (1865) and *Joscelyn* (1867). Simms also worked as an editor for newspapers until his death on June 11, 1870. He is buried in Magnolia Cemetery in Charleston, South Carolina.

THE GRAVE

Simms's memorial is a die, base and cap. His epitaph reads, "Wm Gilmore Simms. Poet. Novelist. Historian. 17th April 1806. 11th June 1870. Not from the bird or beat we take our moral-man only hath the privilege to wear his crown of thorns far nobler than the laurel and wins his immortality from care."

GRAVE REFLECTIONS

Magnolia Cemetery is approximately three miles from the historic district. The rural cemetery includes winding paths with picturesque views of funerary artwork and majestic old oak trees with Spanish moss.

Left: The grave of William Gilmore Simms. *Author's collection.*

Right: A bust of William Gilmore Simms in White Point Garden. *Author's collection.*

Before heading to Magnolia Cemetery, I visited the White Point Garden, a nearly six-acre park with views of Fort Sumter and the Charleston Harbor that is an active black-crowned night heron rookery. Among the old oak trees is a bronze bust of William Gilmore Simms that rests on a granite column inscribed "author, journalist, historian."

Charleston also has the Gateway Walk, a trail that connects several of the city churchyards and gardens. One of my must-sees was the Unitarian Church cemetery that includes a local legend about Poe and a young woman. Poe enlisted in the U.S. Army as a private under the name of Edgar A. Perry. His battery was ordered to Fort Moultrie on Sullivan's Island, South Carolina, and arrived for duty in Charleston on November 18, 1827. As a young soldier, he fell in love with a girl named Annabel Lee whose father disapproved of their courtship and forbade the couple from seeing each other. Annabel would sneak out to the Unitarian cemetery at night to continue her courtship with Private Perry. When the soldier was later transferred, Annabel became sick and died. Her father buried her in this same cemetery where they courted. The father found Perry so disagreeable that he had the gravediggers dig mock graves to confuse the soldier so that he could never properly mourn over the grave of his young love. Poe, who was allegedly this soldier, would go on to compose his famous poem "Annabel Lee" about this young love, whom scholars believe is completely fictional, or about his wife. Poe loved a good story, so I'm repeating it. While I expected to be enchanted by Unitarian Church cemetery, getting caught under a large tree in Circular Congregational Churchyard during a morning rainstorm might have been the most magical part of the entire trip.

27

John M. Daniel

(1825–1865)

Hollywood Cemetery, Richmond, Virginia
Section L, Plot 21
Editor whom Poe once challenged to a duel

I enclose one of the notices—the only one in which the slightest word of disparagement appears. It is written by Daniel—the man whom I challenged when I was here last year.[423]
—Poe

His pen could be a weapon when he saw fit to criticize another. Daniel defended his honor when challenged. When Poe staggered into his newspaper office posing a duel, how could he wound a genius and maintain his reputation?

LIFE BEFORE THE STONE

John Moncure Daniel was born on October 24, 1825, to John Moncure Daniel and Eliza *Mitchell* Daniel in Stafford, Virginia. His great-grandfather Thomas Stone was a signer of the Declaration of Independence. Daniel was educated by his father who was a physician before being sent to school in Richmond, where he lived with his father's uncle.[424] He also studied law with Judge Lomax in Fredericksburg.[425] When he was fourteen, his mother passed away. Just a few years later, in 1844, his father passed away. Daniel could not complete his education, as he now would need to take on the responsibility of caring for his younger brothers.[426] In 1845, he moved to Richmond, where he worked as a librarian of a literary club. Although the position did not pay well, he was able to access a rich collection of texts.[427] He became a contributor to an agricultural monthly, the *Southern Planter*, and was promoted to coeditor the next year. In 1848, the *Richmond Semi-Weekly Examiner* was established, and Daniel became the editor. It would soon become one of the leading papers in the South.[428]

Daniel's criticism was frequently sharp and cutting. Although dueling was outlawed in Virginia in 1810, throughout his editorship, Daniel was challenged to and participated in numerous duels. In the summer of 1848, Poe visited the *Southern Literary Messenger* offices wishing for John R. Thompson to relay a challenge of a duel to Daniel. Thompson refused, and Poe confronted Daniel in person. It is unclear how the men settled the argument since the duel did not take place.[429] Daniel continued to write critical as well as flattering reviews of Poe's work. By 1849, the two were considered friends, and Daniel announced Poe's summer lecture tour in the *Examiner*.

After Poe's death, Daniel wrote an obituary that was published in his paper on October 12, 1849, including a short biography of Poe's life. Daniel also discussed Poe's lecture tour, explaining that "during his last visit, for nearly two months' duration, he has been perfectly himself, neatly dressed, and exceedingly agreeable in his deportment. —He delivered two lectures—worthy of his genius in its best moods."[430] In this obituary, Daniel alluded to Elmira Shelton, writing, "It was universally reported that he was engaged to be married. The lady was a widow, of wealth and beauty, who was an old flame of his, and whom he declared to be the ideal and original of his Lenore."[431]

After Poe's death, Daniel's writing continued to disturb newspaper readers, including when it led to a duel in January 1852 with the editor of the *Richmond Whig*, Edward W. Johnston.[432]

Daniel was appointed as the U.S. diplomat chargé d'affaires in Italy by President Franklin Pierce in July 1853. He was promoted to minister resident in September 1854 and lived in Italy until his diplomatic appointment ended in January 1861.[433] While in Turin, Italy, Daniel wrote a letter to a friend in Richmond that disrupted his social relations when the private details of the letter were shared publicly. Daniel had called the local women ugly along with some disparaging remarks about the noblemen with whom he was associated.[434]

In February 1861, Daniel resumed his position at the *Richmond Semi-Weekly Examiner*.[435] Although he supported Virginia's succession in the Civil War, he did not support Jefferson Davis's decision-making. He joined the war efforts as a staff officer under Major General A.P. Hill and was wounded in June 1862. He continued to be vocal about his displeasure in Davis's selection of generals, and in August 1864, Confederate treasurer Edward C. Elmore took offense and challenged Daniel to a duel. Elmore shot Daniel in the leg.[436]

The grave of John M. Daniel. *Author's collection.*

Daniel contracted tuberculosis and mercury poisoning. After having pneumonia for months, he died on March 30, 1865, and is buried in Hollywood Cemetery.[437]

The Grave

John M. Daniel's grave is an obelisk. His epitaph reads, "In memory of John M. Daniel Son of Dr. John M & Eliza M. Daniel of Strafford Co Virginia and for many years Editor of The Richmond Examiner, Born October 24th 1825, Died March 30th 1865."

Grave Reflections

Not far from Daniel's grave in section K, plot 27 is that of Thomas Ritchie (1778–1854), the founder and editor of the *Richmond Enquirer*. In 1823, Thomas Jefferson wrote, "I read but a single newspaper, Ritchie's Enquirer, the best that is published, or ever has been published in America."[438] Ritchie was called the "Father of Democracy" in Virginia.[439]

28

JOHN REUBEN THOMPSON

(1823–1873)

HOLLYWOOD CEMETERY, RICHMOND, VIRGINIA
SECTION L, PLOT 52
POET AND EDITOR OF THE *SOUTHERN LITERARY MESSENGER*
WHO SPOKE OUT ABOUT POE AFTER DEATH

*Just when I most needed aid and sympathy from them, they turned upon me…
and left me struggling in the mire, unpitied, lonely, desperate. But women do not
argue logically as to one's merits, or demerits: they follow certain heart instincts.
They have been angels of mercy to me, and have tenderly led me from the verge of
ruin while men stood aloof and mocked.*[440]
—*Poe*

Thompson steadily grew to literary fame following in Poe's footsteps by attending the same university, where Thompson was considered the second-best poet who had been educated there, with Poe as the first. Thompson even purchased the newspaper where Poe was once editor and where Poe submitted his work. Thompson may have admired Poe's work, but could he respect his behavior?

LIFE BEFORE THE STONE

John Reuben Thompson was born on October 23, 1823, to John Thompson and Sarah *Dyckman* Thompson in Richmond, Virginia. His family lived at the corner of Fourteenth and Main Streets above his father's hat store. He was educated in Richmond before being sent to Roger's preparatory school in Connecticut. He returned to Richmond, where he studied law for two years before attending the University of Virginia. In 1845, he graduated with the degree of bachelor of laws.[441]

In October 1847, Thompson purchased the *Southern Literary Messenger* and became its editor. It was under Thompson's leadership that Susan Archer Talley would have her poetry published. Thompson continued writing and publishing in other publications, including the *Literary World*, *The International* and *The Knickerbocker*.[442] It was during this time that Edgar A. Poe corresponded with Thompson, requesting copies of the *Messenger*, and proposed writing pieces for it. Thompson would later recount that Poe was intoxicated for two or three weeks. Overall, his impression was not good, and Thompson disapproved of Poe's conduct.[443] During the summer of 1848, Poe visited the *Messenger* offices wanting Thompson to relay a challenge of a duel to John M. Daniel, an editor of the *Semi-Weekly Examiner*. Thompson refused.[444]

The last time that Thompson saw Poe was in September 1849 before Poe's trip north. Poe gave him "Marginalia" and a copy of "Annabel Lee," and Thompson advanced the author a small sum. On September 24, Poe stopped by to see Thompson, who gave him a letter for Rufus Griswold. Thompson recalled that Poe was in high spirits, looking forward to his future.[445] Poe would die within weeks of this last encounter.

Not a decade after Poe's death, his good friend Robert Stanard's death in 1857 left Stanard's wife, Martha Stanard, as a wealthy widow whose home would become a social and intellectual center. She hosted the most coveted literary salon in Richmond. Thompson's work drew in the attention of Martha Stanard; the two became friends, and she became "his Egeria, as she herself was a woman of brilliant intellect whose keen yet sympathetic criticism he constantly sought."[446]

Thompson struggled financially while running the newspaper in Richmond. In 1859, he moved to Georgia, where he became the editor of the *Southern Field and Fireside* after receiving a lucrative salary. His health declined, and he found Augusta, Georgia, altogether disagreeable. He would seek employment elsewhere, and as the Civil War worsened, his anxiety increased and his health deteriorated. He moved to London in 1864, where he became the London correspondent to several American papers.[447]

In 1866, Thompson returned to Richmond but could not find employment. To support himself, he gave lectures on "English Journalism" and "The Life and Genius of Edgar A. Poe." One focus of Thompson's Poe lecture focused on the author's untimely death. While numerous theories were circulating regarding how Poe died, Thompson suggested cooping, a form of election fraud that involved citizens being taken and forced to vote for a particular candidate, frequently several times during one election. As the theory suggests, Poe was kidnapped while in Baltimore, forced to drink alcohol and sent off to vote for a particular candidate. When he returned, his clothes were changed to fool officials so that he could vote again.[448]

In April 1867, Thompson moved to New York. He continued working in various jobs and traveling until 1872. Correspondence from this time shows that his friends knew he was wasting away.[449] By February 1873, his health was so alarming that his friends sent him to Colorado, where he remained until April 17 in hopes that the air would help his tuberculosis. Thompson wanted to head home but realized that he could not make the trip alone. A physician was called. A friend met him in Kansas City and helped him return to New York, where he passed away on April 30, 1873. A funeral was held in New York before his body was sent back to Richmond, where he is buried in Hollywood Cemetery.[450]

The Grave

Thompson's grave is an obelisk with an inscription: "John R. Thompson Born in Richmond, VA. 23, Oct. 1823, Died in New York, 30. April 1873. To the graceful poet, the brilliant Writer, the steadfast friend, the Loyal Virginian, the earnest and consistent Christian. This monument is erected As a token Of admiration and affection By his Northern and Southern Friends."

The grave of John Reuben Thompson. *Author's collection.*

GRAVE REFLECTIONS

I walked by his grave many times, reading this epitaph and wondering who he was. As technology advances, it becomes easier to conduct research via mobile devices. Thompson was beloved by his friends, as noted on his epitaph. As a writer, he is considered polished and graceful. Much of his poetry focuses on the South and the Civil War.

29

SUSAN ARCHER TALLEY WEISS

(1822–1917)

RIVERVIEW CEMETERY, RICHMOND, VIRGINIA
SECTION C-18
POET, FRIEND AND BIOGRAPHER OF QUESTIONABLE FACTS

In fact, if you wish to forget anything upon the spot,
make a note that this thing is to be remembered.[451]
—Poe

Susan Talley was a talented writer who freely exchanged letters with popular writers but whose poetic temperament and deafness may have led to her preference for socializing in smaller groups. She must have been delighted by the thought of Edgar A. Poe visiting her home, Talavera, yet upon his arrival, she found herself overwhelmed by the renowned poet and was frozen in fear. Would she be able to overcome her shyness, nevermore to shy away from intimate conversations in order to befriend the famous poet?

LIFE BEFORE THE STONE

Susan Archer Talley was born on February 14, 1822, in Hanover. Her father studied law and retired to the Richmond area. Her mother was the daughter of Captain Archer of Norfolk.[452] In childhood, she "delighted in all sights and sounds of beauty, and would sit for hours watching the sky in storm and sunshine, or listening to the wind among the trees."[453] At the age of nine, Talley lost her hearing after being ill with scarlet fever.[454] Her parents removed her from school, and Talley began to learn at home, where "her natural love of study deepened into a passion."[455] In an article in December 1859, Talley's deafness is described: "A look, a sign, on their part, or a half-spelled sentence upon the fingers, is instantly caught and interpreted."[456] She was not able to read lips and communicated through written English. Various sources contradict one another in their descriptions of Talley's ability to speak; some state that she continued to speak after becoming deaf, others note that it was difficult for her to speak and in an 1864 letter, it is noted "she was forced to write, for she could not talk."[457] Talley's deafness complicates her biography of Poe in which she portrays herself as a friend and confidante easily conversing with the author and his family members.

Talley's ability to write is unquestioned. In her early teens, she began sharing her poetry with her family. Her rhythmical harmony was commented on, noting that only one other "instance in literary history… under similar circumstances" has occurred, pointing to "James Nack, the deaf and dumb poet of New York."[458] Talley was described as having a life "essentially of a poet" and that she "rarely mingles in society beyond the select circle of friends by whom she is surrounded. She finds her happiness in the quiet pleasures and affections of home."[459] In 1845, her poem "The Spirit of Beauty" was published in the April issue of the *Southern Literary Messenger*, signed "Susan, Richmond."[460] Another poem, "The Gift of Song," was published in the December 1845 issue.[461] Talley would contribute to *Harper's*, *Scribner's* and the *Magnolia Weekly*. Her poetry received positive attention from Poe.[462] In 1848, Poe requested copies of her work that was published in the *Southern Literary Messenger*, writing, "I am not very much mistaken 'Susan' will ere long, stand at the head of

American poetesses. She has, in fact, more real genius than all of them put together."[463] And she was included in Rufus Griswold's *The Female Poets of America*.[464] Poe was pleased to see her work included, noting, "I am glad to see that Griswold, although imperfectly, has done her justice in his late 'Female Poets of America.'"[465]

During the summer of 1849, Poe was on a lecture tour to raise money for his magazine *The Stylus*. Talley's home, Talavera, was near the house of Elmira *Royster* Shelton, whom Poe was courting before his fateful trip to Baltimore. Poe visited Talavera in July 1849 with his sister, Rosalie, and would visit the home throughout that summer. On his first visit, Talley was so shy and overwhelmed in the presence of the renowned poet that she left it to the other women to entertain Poe as Talley kept her distance.[466] The prior November 1848, she had corresponded freely with Poe.[467] In her biography of Poe, Talley, who clearly had become more comfortable in Poe's company, recounted how one rainy morning Poe asked her to review and help edit his poem, "The Raven." She recalled:

> *His first intention, he said, had been to write a short poem only, based upon the incident of an Owl—a night-bird, the bird of wisdom—with its ghostly presence and inscrutable gaze entering the window of a vault or chamber where he sat beside the bier of the lost Lenore. Then he had exchanged the Owl for the Raven, for the sake of the latter's "Nevermore."*[468]

Talley joined Rosalie and Mrs. Mackenzie in attending Poe's Richmond lecture on August 17, 1849, and again Talley and Rosalie attended his lecture on September 24, 1849. During this second lecture, Elmira *Royster* Shelton was in the audience. Just before leaving Richmond in late September 1849, Poe gave a private reading at Talavera, where he recited "The Raven" for the last time.[469]

After Poe's death, Talley, who became a Confederate spy during the Civil War, was arrested for carrying messages in the braids of her hair.[470] Her aid to the Confederate troops escalated when she attempted to transport a coffin full of percussion primers through the enemy lines. When stopped, she stated that her brother's body was in the coffin, but as soon as the lid was lifted, Talley was taken under arrest.[471] While imprisoned at Fort McHenry, Talley met and secretly married a Union solider, Lieutenant Louis Von Weiss, on May 13, 1862.[472] A difference in opinion led to her filing for divorce and suing for custody of their only child, Stuart Archer Weiss. She refused alimony and supported herself and her son by writing.[473]

The family grave of Susan Archer Talley Weiss. *Author's collection.*

In 1907, her biography of Poe, *The Home Life of Poe*, was published by Broadway Publishing Company of New York.[474] On April 7, 1917, she died at her home in Richmond.[475] She was ninety-five years old and is buried in Riverview Cemetery.

THE GRAVE

The monument for Susan Archer *Talley* Weiss is a die, base and cap headstone. The Weiss grave marker includes Susan Archer *Talley* Weiss along with her son, Stuart Archer Weiss. The back of the grave includes an epitaph for the author's mother, Eliza Francis Archer, and the author's brother, Robert Archer Talley.

GRAVE REFLECTIONS

Approximately two miles from the cemetery is Talavera, the only house still standing in Richmond where Poe once visited. Built in 1838, the house is a private residence. Tucked away on a quiet street, one might wish to take a stroll by the house while reciting "The Raven." *2315 West Grace Street | Richmond, Virginia*

159

30

Susan V.C. Ingram

(1831–1917)

ELMWOOD CEMETERY, NORFOLK, VIRGINIA
MAIN CENTER, LOT 69
FRIEND WHO RECEIVED A PERSONAL COPIED MANUSCRIPT
OF THE POEM "ULALUME"

I am sure I would do anything else at your bidding.
—Poe

Susan Ingram could not imagine a more enchanted evening with the infamous Edgar Allan Poe reciting to her small circle of family and friends. She must have felt how the skies would become "ashen and sober" and how the leaves would soon become crisp and dry in the next month as she listened to the poetry, but it was still September, and during that moonlight recitation, she could not imagine a more perfect moment—until the next day, when she received a note from the poet. Had he actually transcribed the poem she had admired?

LIFE BEFORE THE STONE

Susan V.C. Ingram was born in 1831 to Dr. John Ingram and Mary L.E. Ingram in the former Princess Anne County, Virginia, which is now part of the city of Virginia Beach. She was the third daughter in the family. When she was just a toddler, the eldest daughter, Sarah Ann Livingston Ingram, died. Susan remained close to her sister, Mary Celestia. In 1844, her brother, John H., was born.

During the summer of 1849, Poe went on a lecture tour to raise money for his magazine. He went to Philadelphia, Richmond and Norfolk. On Sunday, September 9, 1849, while at the Hygeia Hotel at Old Point in Norfolk, Susan Ingram and her sister, Mary C., who were the guests of their cousin Susan Maxwell and aunt Mrs. D. French became part of a small party who hosted Poe. While gathered on the veranda, Ingram's aunt noted, "This seems to be just the time and place for poetry, Mr. Poe." Ingram recalled:

> We all felt it. The old Hygeia stood some distance from the water, but with nothing between it and the ocean. It was moonlight and the light shone over everything with that undimmed light that it has in the South....Our little party was absolutely cut off from everything except that lovely view of the water shining in the moonlight and its gentle music borne to us on the soft breeze. Poe felt the influence....And when we seconded the request that he recite for us he agreed readily.[476]

Years later, Ingram's recollections show that she was enchanted by that evening of the poet reciting "The Raven" and "Annabel Lee." The day after the recitation, Ingram received a handwritten copy of a poem along with a letter from Poe, "I have transcribed 'Ulalume' with much pleasure, dear Miss Ingram—as I am sure I would do anything else at your bidding."[477]

After that magical evening, Ingram recalled that Poe visited her family's home outside of Norfolk, where they discussed their fondness for orris root, a floral and earthy fragrance with a violet, pepper and raspberry profile. Ingram always had it on her clothing; the fragrance reminded Poe of his foster mother, Frances Valentine Allan.[478]

The year 1849 was an exciting one for the Ingram daughters. However, the realities of daily life returned the following year, as their mother died in 1850. Their brother was just a boy, and the sisters now faced new responsibilities in the household.

On June 6, 1855, Mary C. Ingram married Charles N. Bosher of Richmond, Virginia. Susan did not marry. Both daughters lived long lives. Mary Bosher passed in 1909, and Susan Ingram passed in 1917. Ingram is buried in Elmwood Cemetery.

While Ingram kept fond memories throughout her lifetime of her visits with Poe, she regrettably misplaced her copy of "Ulalume" and her letter from Poe.[479] The copy and the letter were later purchased by Pierpont Morgan and are in the Morgan Library in New York.[480]

The grave of Susan V.C. Ingram. *Author's collection.*

THE GRAVE

Susan V.C. Ingram's grave is a small die in socket with her name, birth and death years. Her grave is part of a family plot with her parents and siblings, including her sister Mary Celestia Bosher.

GRAVE REFLECTIONS

The first time I visited Elmwood Cemetery was in 2017. River City Cemetarians joined the Strange Happenings Tour by Norfolk Society for Cemetery Conservation. Our guide, Josh, was amazing. Norfolk folks came out in masses, and several dressed quite fashionably to get into the spirit. Those on the tour were fortunate enough to enter the grandiose John Core Mausoleum with its Greek Revival architecture and Egyptian motifs. It was a rare treat to see the artwork up close. In 1915, the construction of the mausoleum cost $100,000.[481] Today, it would cost millions to recreate.

31

Sarah Elmira Royster Shelton

(1810–1888)

Shockoe Hill Cemetery, Richmond, Virginia
Range 7, Section 2, near the corner of Second and
Hospital Streets
First and last fiancée of Edgar Allan Poe

I think she loves me more devotedly than any one I ever knew.
—Poe

He was attractive and clever, and although he would soon head to Jefferson's university, he promised to write her. How could she not fall for the young poet? But those letters were blocked by her father, and she married another. Decades later, she was a widow and he a widower, and he still wanted her hand in marriage. She yielded to his every request, but couldn't they postpone the marriage by a few months? Poe headed to Baltimore, and a wedding announcement was replaced with an obituary.

LIFE BEFORE THE STONE

Sarah Elmira Royster was born about 1810 into a wealthy family in Richmond, Virginia, as the eldest child to James Royster and Mary Gregory *Bohannan* Royster. Her sister, Lucy Ann, was born in 1811; her brother James Bohannon was born in 1814, and Alexander L. was born in 1817. Her father had invested in the Ellis & Allan firm, and their family lived on Fifth Street along with the Allans, Poe's foster family.[482]

During the summer of 1825, when Elmira was fifteen years old, she became the focus of a handsome young poet who was smart and romantic. She fell for the teenage Poe. His foster father called him "sulky."[483] Elmira would later reminisce that he had been a "beautiful boy [who was] not very talkative… [and] his general manner was sad."[484] Elmira and Edgar spent a good amount of time together as teens. They played piano together and took longs walks, escaping into gardens to avoid judgmental glances. Elmira attended a Sunday church service with Edgar and his foster mother, Frances Allan.[485] And she even met his brother, Henry Poe. In March 1825, the University of Virginia opened, and Poe, who was an eager, capable learner, wanted a university education. Allan assisted Poe in obtaining an early entrance into the university. Just weeks after turning seventeen, Poe registered for the second session on February 14, 1826.[486] The distance of seventy miles must have seemed an impossible distance. Before leaving, Elmira and Edgar were secretly engaged. Poe promised to write, and while he kept his word, she never had the chance to read any of his musings or promises of love.

When the first letters arrived from Poe to Elmira, James Royster seized them. He must have thought his daughter could do better than an alliance with a penniless orphan. Even though the Allans spared no expense in raising Poe, he had never been adopted and would not be certain to inherit any money. Elmira would later state that her father intercepted the letters because he believed they simply were too young for such a serious commitment.[487]

Poe struggled while at the university, not because he was academically incapable—he simply did not have the finances that his peers had. Poe could not pay all the bills required of a university education and tried gambling to better his chances of paying his bills; instead, he incurred more debt and disappointed his foster father, who disapproved of gambling. Poe left the university, returning to the family home on December 21, 1826.

Once home, Poe argued with his foster father and was completely deflated about his career at the University of Virginia ending. He also had not received any letters from his betrothed and soon discovered that she was now engaged to another man. It would have been easier for Poe to wallow in hopelessness, but even as a teen, he persevered and would write through the pain.

On December 6, 1828, Reverend Stephen Taylor married the eighteen-year-old Elmira Royster to the twenty-one-year-old Alexander Barrett Shelton, a prosperous man her family chose as a more suitable match. Outwardly, the couple appeared to be an excellent pair. Their first daughter, Ann Elizabeth Shelton, was born on February 6, 1830. As Elmira was starting her own family with her husband, her father died on May 10, 1833. She devoted herself to her religion, and at the age of twenty-four, she was baptized at St. John's Episcopal Church.[488]

Around 1836, Elmira and Poe's paths crossed. She would later recall:

> *I remember seeing Edgar, & his lovely wife, very soon after they were married—I met them—I never shall forget my feelings at the time— They were indescribable, almost agonizing—However in an instant, I remembered that I was a married woman, and banished them from me, as I would a poisonous reptile.*[489]

In January 1838, a second daughter, Sarah Elmira Shelton, was born to Elmira and her husband. Sadly, the baby died on June 18, 1840. Her first son, Southall B. Shelton, was born in 1839. He and his sister, Ann Elizabeth, would have full lives. In 1843, their second son, Alexander Barret Shelton Jr., was born. He would pass away within a few years and was buried on February 2, 1848. That same year, her husband, who is said to have leaped into the James River to save a drowning man, passed away on July 12 due to pneumonia.[490] Elmira and her children were left an inheritance with the stipulation that if she were to remarry, she would lose a portion of the estate. She focused on her children, especially on October 17, 1848, when her daughter, Ann Elizabeth, married John Henry Leftwich.[491]

In late July 1849, Poe reunited with Shelton, first stopping by her home in Church Hill. He was in Richmond on his lecture tour and planned to sell some essays to the *Southern Literary Messenger*. Elmira had not seen him in quite some time, and she was on her way to church. She could not be delayed but told him to call again. When he returned, she learned that after two decades, he hoped to renew their engagement. It had only been a year since her husband passed, and she felt she needed time to consider such a proposal. She was no longer the naïve teen Poe once knew, but Poe did not wish to wait. Elmira recalled, "He said a love that hesitated was not a love for him."[492] Elmira acquiesced. Poe had a specific vision for how his life would be with Elmira. He planned to bring his aunt and mother-in-law, Maria Clemm, to Richmond to live with them so they would have housing security. He also planned to educate Elmira's son, Southall, himself, which would save them money. Plans were moving ahead, yet Poe continued to think about Annie Richmond, a married woman he had met the year before in Massachusetts. Elmira's family, especially her daughter, were not in support of the marriage.

It is hard not to question Poe's motives or read anything romantic into this reengagement with Elmira after reading his August 29, 1849 letter to Maria Clemm. Poe's letter focused on Shelton's money; his love for Annie, stating, "I worship her beyond all human love"; and finding a secure home for Clemm and himself. Elmira's hesitation infuriated Poe. He wrote, "I got angry with her for wishing to defer [the wedding] till January & wrote her a cross letter."[493] Poe's description of Elmira as "amiable, gentle, domestic, and affectionate" evokes more of a mother figure than a romantic partner. He admired her ability to manage her money, explaining, "Mr. Shelton left property to the amount of $60,000, and since his death it has much increased in value and is now worth at least 70,000," when Poe did not have a keen eye for business. He undercharged for tickets to his Richmond lecture, which included "a crowded house (250 persons)" and even managed to owe more money than he made.[494] Regardless of the seeming lack of passion, Poe must have liked a woman who "cordially agrees to all that [he] propose[d]."[495] There was also a good amount of nostalgia regarding their courtship when they were teens. And while without enough money to pay his hotel bill, he bought Elmira a gold locket that included a lock of his hair, a wedding ring and a daguerreotype of himself.[496]

On September 26, 1849, Elmira and Poe spent the evening together before he headed north. She shared:

> *He was very sad, and complained of being quite sick. I felt his pulse, and found he had considerable fever, and did not think it probable he would be able to start the next morning as he anticipated. I felt so wretched about him all that night, that I went up early the next morning to inquire after him, when, much to my regret, he had left in the boat for Baltimore.*[497]

After leaving Shelton's home, he made a stop at Dr. John Carter's and then headed north, stopping in Baltimore, where he would pass away on October 3, 1849. While on his deathbed, Poe said that "he had a wife in Richmond," which presumably was his fiancée, Elmira Shelton.[498]

Elmira learned of Poe's death in the newspaper. She wrote to Maria Clemm,

> *I have not been able to get any of the particulars of his sickness & death, except an extract from the* Baltimore Sun, *which said that he died on Sunday, the 7th of this month, with congestion of the brain, after an illness of 7 days.*[499]

Although they had not been officially married, Elmira wore mourning clothing and stated, "[Poe] was dearer to me than any other living creature."[500]

Elmira Shelton continued living in Church Hill. On February 14, 1858, her mother, Mary Gregory Royster, passed and was buried in the same graveyard as Poe's mother—St. John's Churchyard.

Shelton's son fought in the Civil War and lost an eye. Like most Southerners', her finances were depleted after the war. She moved to Ashland to live with her daughter and her daughter's husband. By 1875, Shelton had moved back to Richmond and was living on Clay Street. That year, she was interviewed by Edward Valentine, who was a Richmond sculptor whose family established The Valentine Museum. At the time Shelton spoke with Valentine, she denied being engaged, but then nearly a decade later, in June 1884, she admitted to the physician who was there during Poe's death that she had been engaged.[501]

On February 11, 1888, Elmira died and is buried by her husband in Shockoe Hill Cemetery.

THE GRAVE

Elmira Shelton is buried next to her husband, whose marker is a table tombstone. In September 2012, a plaque was placed on her grave that reads:

Sarah Elmira Royster Shelton
1810–1888
First and last fiancée of the poet Edgar Allan Poe
"She was a child and I was a child
In this kingdom by the sea.
We loved with a love that was more than love—
I and my Annabel Lee—"
—Edgar A. Poe

Plaque at the grave of Sarah Elmira Royster Shelton. *Author's collection.*

The graves of Elmira Shelton and Alexander Barrett Shelton. *Author's collection.*

GRAVE REFLECTIONS

Each time I visit Shockoe Hill Cemetery, which is often, I visit Elmira Shelton's grave. Her grave is in section 2, in a shady area off the path. The terrain is uneven. Alexander Barrett Shelton's table tomb grave is in remarkable condition. While the epitaph is illegible, the gravestone stands with no visual signs of structural damage. The table tomb is usually lined in stones, a tradition noting the grave has been visited, which is more likely a tribute to Elmira than to her husband. I admit that I always question how Mr. Shelton might have felt had he known his wife's marker would note that she was a fiancée of another man.

32

Dr. John F. Carter

(1825–1905)

Shockoe Hill Cemetery, Richmond, Virginia
Range 13, Section 8
Doctor and Poe's friend

Mysteries force a man to think, and so injure his health.[502]
—*Poe*

The group noted that an audience of thirteen was a bad omen, although they were more frustrated at the apathy in the low number in attendance. A young Dr. John F. Carter was delighted to see Poe recite his poems; he would carry these memories throughout his life. On the poet's final evening in Richmond, would his sword cane be returned?

Life Before the Stone

Dr. John F. Carter was born in Richmond, Virginia, on September 6, 1825, to William Carter Jr. and Mary *Gibbon* Carter.[503] He trained to become a physician, which would be his profession throughout his lifetime.

Dr. Carter became friends with Poe during the author's lecture tour in 1849. Dr. Carter, who was twenty-four years old at the time, was a friend of Jane Mackenzie and Rosalie Poe. It was at the Mackenzie home where Carter first heard Poe recite "The Raven" and "Annabel Lee." That August, Carter also accompanied other friends of Poe to the Exchange concert room where Poe gave a public recital to a group of thirteen people. Susan Archer Talley Weiss was in the audience.[504]

Dr. Carter lived between Duncan Lodge and Elmira Royster Shelton's home. On Poe's last night in Richmond, he stopped in to see Carter at his office at 9:30 p.m. The two sat around talking while Poe played with Carter's Malacca sword cane a friend had given him. Poe announced that he was going to go over to the restaurant Saddler's. As Poe left, he took the sword cane that belonged to Carter, leaving his own cane behind. When Carter had not heard back from Poe, he contacted Saddler's to learn that Poe had left around midnight with a group he had met at the restaurant with the intention of heading to the Baltimore boat since it was scheduled to leave at 4:00 a.m. Poe left behind his baggage in his room at the Swan Tavern.[505] Carter's cane was only returned to him after Poe's death on October 7, 1849. Carter, however, kept Poe's cane as a memento of their friendship; after Carter's death, the cane was passed down to friends and their family members. Poe's cane was finally presented to the Poe Museum in 1923.[506]

In 1852, Carter married Louisa Rhodes, and together the couple would have four children, with one dying as a baby.[507] While his life moved on, he never forgot about his connection to the poet. Soon the country was swept up with the Civil War. On July 30, 1862, Carter enlisted as a private. He was discharged that October. He continued as a surgeon and was "a physician in charge of the smallpox hospital of Camp Lee." Like many Virginians during the Civil War, his farm was raided, and he lost much of his property.[508]

In Carter's later years, he had "long gray hair and flowing whiskers [and] he was a natural for a Santa Claus."[509] He continued to share memories of his connection to Poe and even acquired an authentic photograph of Poe for which the author sat, not a duplicate. He received the photograph from Poe's sister.[510] After having heart issues, his wife, Louisa Rhodes Carter, died on November 25, 1901. Carter passed on September 1, 1905. He is buried beside his wife in Shockoe Hill Cemetery.

THE GRAVE

Dr. John F. Carter has a small headstone that is worn. The epitaph reads, "Dr. John F. Carter / Died / September 1, 1905 / Aged 80 years."

The grave of John Carter. *Author's collection.*

GRAVE REFLECTIONS

One of the enjoyments of research is making connections between individuals. While death announcements can make me a bit sad, obituaries usually delight me because I learn more about the life of the individual. When I saw the death announcement of Augusta *Carter* Minnigerode, the daughter of Dr. Carter and Louisa Rhodes Carter, I quickly did a search to determine that her husband, Lewis D. Minnigerode, was the son of Dr. Charles Frederick Ernest Minnigerode, the German-born College of William & Mary professor who introduced the German custom of the Christmas tree to Williamsburg. I have stood at both Dr. Carter's grave in Shockoe Hill and Dr. Minnigerode's grave in Hollywood many times over the years. Now I get to connect the two individuals, since they were united by the marriage of their children. On further research, I learned that Dr. Carter was also the brother of Mary *Carter* Minnigerode, the wife of Dr. Charles Frederick Ernest Minnigerode.

33

Joseph Evans Snodgrass

(1813–1880)

I sincerely thank you for the interest you have taken in my well-doing.
The friendship of a man of talent, who is at the same time a man of honorable
feeling, is especially valuable in these days of double dealing.
I hope I shall always deserve your good opinion.[511]
—Poe

Snodgrass encouraged wearing the blue-ribbon badge of the temperance movement. Was it his strong beliefs or his memory that could sometimes lead to blurry facts? His politics increased readership. His peer swore off liquor, so why was his face so haggard and his clothing so tousled?

LIFE BEFORE THE STONE

Joseph Evans Snodgrass was born on August 8, 1813, the youngest child to Robert Snodgrass and Catherine Thomas *Evans* Snodgrass near Berkeley Springs, Virginia, now Hedgesville, West Virginia. The area was originally settled by his great-grandfather William Snodgrass around 1700 but not officially established until 1836, the year Joseph married his wife, Hannah Chandlee.[512] That year, he also received his medical degree from the University of Maryland.[513] Snodgrass wrote poems and essays for *Burton's*,

Graham's, Godey's and the *Southern Literary Messenger*.[514] The couple settled in Baltimore, Maryland.

By this point, Snodgrass and Poe were already acquaintances and exchanging letters that were mostly focused on writing and other business. Snodgrass and Nathan C. Brooks served as editors of *American Museum of Science, Literature, and the Arts*, where Poe contributed "Ligeia" in September 1838.[515] The poem "The Haunted Palace" would be published in the April 1839 issue.[516]

Snodgrass became proprietor of the *Saturday Visiter* in the early 1840s. In one letter on April 1, 1841, from Philadelphia, Poe thanked Snodgrass for defending his reputation. Poe shared with Snodgrass, a proponent of the temperance movement:

> *At no period of my life was I ever what men call intemperate. I never was in the habit of intoxication....For a brief period, while I resided in Richmond, and edited the* Messenger, *I certainly did give way, at long intervals, to the temptation held out on all sides by the spirit of Southern conviviality. My sensitive temperament could not stand an excitement which was an everyday matter to my companions. In short, it sometimes happened that I was completely intoxicated.*[517]

In October 1842, Snodgrass attended Lucretia Mott's lecture on the evils of slavery. He began including more antislavery pieces in the *Visiter*.[518] The first powerful emancipationist essay was during the summer of 1843. In a private letter, Snodgrass shared that he had lost a few subscribers but "gained a great many" throughout the South.[519]

Snodgrass continued producing the literary magazine and published various writing. In 1848, his focus turned to family with the birth of their son, Stanley Starr Snodgrass. While the birth of a child was joyful, the next year, Snodgrass became a key player in the final days of Poe's death.

On October 3, 1849, Snodgrass received an urgent message from a printer named Joseph Walker who requested his aid on behalf of Poe. Although the original note no longer exists, a literature professor transcribed it. Walker wrote, "There is a gentleman, rather the worse for wear...who appears in great distress."[520] Snodgrass went to Ryan's inn, which was also called Gunner's Hall and functioned as a tavern that also included rooms. On this day, it was also used as a polling place. At some point, Poe must have shared that Snodgrass was an acquaintance. Some scholars argue that Poe shared the name Snodgrass over his Baltimore relatives as Poe may have stopped in the city on his way north "to renew literary ties."[521] Snodgrass lived close by and was able to meet his old peer. Noticing that Poe was unwell and out of sorts, Snodgrass reserved a room in the tavern, but Henry Herring, who had been married to Poe's aunt Elizabeth *Poe* Herring arrived only to suggest that the hospital might be a better place to take Poe. Herring cited past incidents when an intoxicated Poe was an unwelcome houseguest. Poe was sent to the Washington Medical College hospital, where he was under the care of Dr. John J. Moran for the next four days before dying on October 7, 1849.[522] Snodgrass was one of the few who attended Poe's funeral on that chilling October day.

Snodgrass wrote several different accounts of Poe's final days, beginning in the 1856 issue of *Women's Temperance Paper*. Recounting from memory, Snodgrass is often criticized by scholars for misrepresenting several facts in those final days. Ironically, in Poe's "Chapter on Autography," Poe wrote about Snodgrass, "His chirography is bad—stiff, sprawling and illegible, with frequent corrections and interlineations, evincing inactivity not less than fastidiousness. The signature betrays a meretricious love of effect."[523] It is significant to note that Snodgrass as both an editor and writer must have always had his *audience* in mind when writing. Seven years after Poe's death, Snodgrass *remembered* that the Walker note included that Poe was "in a state of beastly intoxication and evident destitution," which perhaps was more Snodgrass's recollection on seeing Poe or what he believed the audience would wish to read, as the note did not include that phrasing.[524] Those final days stayed with him even if his memory of the exact events faded. He wrote another account of Poe's final days for *Beadle's Monthly* (March 1867) and a poem published in the *Baltimorean* (November 1875), in which Snodgrass shared that the funeral "haunts [him] still."[525]

Snodgrass passed away on May 24, 1880, and is buried in Mount Zion churchyard, now called Hedgesville Cemetery. Oddly enough, his cousin had been interred in his plot "by mistake." Snodgrass's will requested that his cousin's remains be transferred so that he could be in his original plot beside his father.[526]

THE GRAVE

The headstone reads: "In memory of Dr. Joseph E. Snodgrass born in Berkeley, West Va. August 8, 1813. Died May 24, 1880. Our departed friend was a man whose real motives were too often misunderstood by his sincere friends in public affairs."

Left: The grave of Dr. Joseph E. Snodgrass. *Author's collection.*

Below: The Snodgrass family plot. *Author's collection.*

Grave Reflections

I visited Hedgesville Cemetery on a beautiful day. His grave was easy to locate, as it is one of few within a fenced plot. The fence is ornamental, which surprised me, since in his will, Snodgrass requested "that the expenditures for his funeral shall be the least possible sum consistent with the customs of the neighborhood" and that he wished "no plate on his coffin."[527]

34

Elizabeth Rebecca Herring Tutt Smith

(1815–1889)

You cannot imagine how much we have all missed you.
It seems as if we had lost one of our family—but I believe it is always the way
in this world—we never know the true value of our friends until Death
or Distance deprives us of their society.[528]
—Poe

Lovely and kind, Elizabeth Rebecca captured the attention of several hearts. She knew her own share of love and loss. How could she imagine the significance of the verses added to her album by her cousin?

Life Before the Stone

Elizabeth Rebecca Herring was born on October 13, 1815, in Baltimore, Maryland, to Elizabeth *Poe* Herring and Henry Herring, who worked as a lumber dealer.[529] As a young teenager, her cousin Poe visited her and wrote an acrostic poem spelling out Elizabeth Rebecca in her album. Sometimes called friendship albums, these early nineteenth-century books were usually owned by "young white women on the cusp of adulthood."[530] The albums, which were often leather-bound books, served as tangible ways to remember relationships and for friends to leave sentimental compliments. The inscriptions were not often original compositions, so Elizabeth Herring

The grave of Elizabeth R. Herring Smith in Loudon Park Cemetery rests on the hill to the right of the tree. *Author's collection.*

must have been pleased to have original poems written by her cousin. Poe also gave her a copy of his published collection *Al Aaraaf, Tamerlane and Minor Poems*. Around 1833, he also wrote "To Elizabeth" in one of her albums. This poem, titled "Lines Written in an Album" would later be published in the September 1835 issue of the *Southern Literary Messenger* and dedicated to Eliza White, the daughter of the newspaper owner.[531]

On December 2, 1834, she married Andrew Turner Tutt, who died of tuberculosis within a year on November 19, 1835. In an 1842 letter from Poe to Elizabeth, he wrote about his wife Virginia's health, their move to another home in Philadelphia and that he had "resigned editorship of 'Graham's Magazine.'"[532] In the 1840s, she married Edmund Smith, who worked as the headmaster of a school in Baltimore. In 1845, Elizabeth loaned Poe a volume of his poems to be used as a "printer's copy" for *The Raven and Other Poems*. In 1846, the first of their children, Edmund Morton Smith II, was born. That same year, she visited Poe at Fordham when both he and Virginia were quite ill. In January 1847, Virginia died.

Elizabeth and her husband were part of the few who attended Poe's funeral in 1849. Her father paid for Poe's mahogany coffin. The ceremony was short, perhaps due to the dreary October weather.[533]

Elizabeth's husband died in 1863, making her a widow for the second time. She died on October 17, 1889, and is buried in Loudon Park Cemetery.

The Grave

Elizabeth Herring's is a broken tab in socket. The tablet portion rests on the ground. It reads "Elizabeth R. Herring, wife of Edmund Smith, born October 18, 1815, died, October 17, 1889. / At Rest." It does not appear to be part of a family plot; a broken marker missing the top tablet rests beside it.

Grave Reflections

Elizabeth's marker rests on a lovely hillside in the cemetery away from congested family plots. It was a gorgeous March day when I visited.

The grave of Elizabeth R. Herring Smith. *Author's collection.*

Although I knew the grave's section, it required a bit of hunting. When I found her marker, a local church's noon church bells began playing "Ave Maria."

Her parents are buried approximately six miles away in Old St. Paul's Cemetery, a 2.4-acre walled burial ground that was opened in 1802. It is one of the oldest cemeteries, organized a few years after Baltimore was incorporated as a city. The cemetery is included on the National Register of Historic Places. Francis Scott Key, best known for writing the lyrics for the national anthem "The Star-Spangled Banner," was originally buried here but later was disinterred and moved to a family plot in Frederick, Maryland. The cemetery remains locked and open by appointments only. I tried for over a month to gain access before determining that if I included that cemetery in this collection it would only lead others to similar frustrations when attempting to visit.

35

NEILSON POE

(1809–1884)

Neilson Poe at 34

GREEN MOUNT CEMETERY, BALTIMORE, MARYLAND
OUTLINE AREA 1
LAWYER AND POE'S COUSIN

*In your private ear, I believe him to be the bitterest enemy I have in the world.
He is the more despicable in this, since he makes loud professions of friendship.*[534]
—Poe

Neilson Poe was first a journalist before becoming a lawyer and judge.
Would his cousin make their family name known to the world? Neilson
had a prosperous life and family although his cousin believed him to be
jealous of his success. He quietly paid for the hearse, not knowing what
would come of the death narrative.

LIFE BEFORE THE STONE

Neilson Poe and his twin sister, Amelia Fitzgerald Poe, were born on August 11, 1809, in Baltimore, Maryland, to Jacob Poe and Bridget Amelia Fitzgerald *Kennedy* Poe. His father was a well-known merchant in the city. By eighteen, Neilson Poe had entered the office of William Gwynn, proprietor of the *Federal Gazette and Baltimore Daily Advertiser*. He worked there as a writer for three years. In 1830, he became the owner and editor of the *Frederick Examiner*.[535] That year, in a letter to his cousin and future wife, Josephine Emily Clemm, Neilson Poe shared that Edgar had published poetry and that this would lead to their family name becoming well known.[536] Neilson Poe stayed at the *Frederick Examiner* for four years before moving to Baltimore.[537]

On November 30, 1831, Neilson Poe married Josephine Emily Clemm.[538] They started their family and would have five sons and two daughters. Neilson's reputation grew "as an elegant, graceful and forcible writer."[539] In 1834, he took control of the *Baltimore Chronicle*, where he would continue until 1840, when he quit journalism to focus on practicing law.[540] During his time at the *Chronicle*, Neilson Poe offered to take in Virginia and Maria Clemm, with plans of offering secure housing and an education for Virginia, most likely considering her too young to marry.[541] This offer infuriated Poe, who wrote to his aunt, "I am blinded with tears while writing this letter," asking his aunt to "take pity on [him]" and wishing to beg "Virginia! do not go!"[542] In October 1839, Edgar even wrote a friend that Neilson was his "bitterest enemy," and shared, "I cannot account for his hostility except in being vain enough to imagine him jealous of the little literary reputation I have, of late years, obtained. But enough of the little dog."[543] By the mid-1840s, letters between the cousins show Edgar's attitude toward Neilson having softened, even if it was to be cordial.

In 1842, after having left journalism, Neilson became the director on the part of the state in the Baltimore and Ohio Railroad Company. After his term ended, Neilson returned to practicing law.[544]

In October 1849, Edgar's friend Dr. Joseph Snodgrass and his uncle Henry Herring called a carriage to take Poe to Washington Medical College after finding him in what they thought was a drunken stupor.[545] Dr. Moran, the doctor who was overseeing Edgar A. Poe's treatment, contacted Neilson regarding his cousin's health.[546] Once Neilson arrived at the hospital, the doctor on duty believed Edgar was too excitable to have a visitor so Neilson sent in some linens and decided to return to the hospital the next day. The details of Edgar A. Poe's final moments are dreadful. He was in a state of madness and cried out the name "Reynolds" numerous times. Scholars argue over the identity of the man in question, and some believe that the name was misheard.[547] Edgar Poe died on October 7, 1849, and was buried on October 8 at 4:00 p.m.

Neilson Poe was tasked with making the final arrangements for Edgar Allan Poe. While deaths are not typically planned, Neilson Poe was a cousin, so it is not that surprising that with poor weather and the awkward circumstances, the funeral did not have any hints of ceremony today's Poe fans might expect. Henry Herring provided a mahogany coffin, while Neilson paid for the hearse for the funeral.[548] The tragedy of Poe's death did not end at the time of his demise. Neilson provided a marble headstone to mark his cousin's grave, but that was destroyed in the marble yard before making its way to the churchyard, which left the poet's grave unmarked for the next few decades.[549] During these final preparations and correspondence among family, Dr. Moran discovered the whereabouts of Edgar Poe's trunk and shipped it to Neilson Poe, presumably seeing him as the next of kin. Neilson also had the burden of confirming the truth of Poe's death to family members who read announcements in newspapers. Neilson responded to Maria Clemm confirming that Edgar Poe had indeed passed away.[550] While scholars point to the hastiness of the final arrangements, Neilson made these preparations while continuing his law practice and tending to his own family. There may not have been much pomp and circumstance in the ceremony, but Neilson Poe's life was considered "modest and refined, and in his home no man was ever more gracious or beloved."[551] Further, unlike many other family members and friends of Poe, Neilson Poe "never used the death narrative for the purposes of self-promotion or profit once Poe's fame grew."[552]

Neilson Poe continued working in his law practice until 1879, when he was elected as a court judge and commissioned as chief judge. He was chief judge of the Orphan's Court in Baltimore until 1884.[553] He declined reelection based on his health.[554]

In his final years, his health failed, and on January 3, 1889, at 7:00 p.m., Neilson Poe died in Baltimore. He is buried in Green Mount Cemetery near his son Robert M. Poe, who died five years before.

The grave of Neilson Poe. *Author's collection.*

THE GRAVE

Neilson Poe's gravestone is a die in socket that he shares with his wife. The top of the headstone includes a cross. It reads, "Neilson Poe Born August 11, 1809 / Died Jan. 3. 1884" before including details of his wife's birth and death. At the bottom, the marker reads, "Blessed are the pure in heart for they shall see God."

GRAVE REFLECTIONS

I visited Neilson Poe's grave on my second visit to Green Mount. It was a gorgeous spring day, and there were several groups walking through the cemetery with maps, which I'm partial to over phone apps. Whenever I visit a cemetery that offers a map, I always take one and keep it. If I can buy a stylized map that helps support the efforts of conservation in a cemetery, that's even better. Yet I also love to meander through the paths while looking at markers, trees and wildlife. This is when I find the best places for reflection.

36

ZACCHEUS COLLINS LEE

(1805–1859)

CONGRESSIONAL CEMETERY, WASHINGTON, D.C.
SECTION 2, RANGE 27, SITE 170
JURIST AND POE'S CLASSMATE AND FRIEND
WHO ATTENDED HIS FUNERAL

Out—out are the lights—out all!
And, over each quivering form,
The curtain, a funeral pall,
Comes down with the rush of a storm,
And the angels, all pallid and wan,
Uprising, unveiling, affirm
That the play is the tragedy, "Man,"
And its hero the Conqueror Worm.[555]
—Poe

Z. Collins Lee was a man of integrity and honor who had a kind heart. He was an eloquent speaker who was frequently called on to say a few words at various events. On that cold October day, what words would he conjure for his old classmate?

LIFE BEFORE THE STONE

Zaccheus Collins Lee was born in Fairfax, Virginia, on December 5, 1805, to Richard Bland Lee and Elizabeth *Collins* Lee. His father was of the prominent Lee family and was a planter, jurist and politician. Z. Collins Lee was one of nine children and a first cousin to Robert E. Lee, who would become a general for the Confederacy during the Civil War.

From an early age, Z. Collins Lee was fond of "belles-lettres reading."[556] By 1825, he was a student in the junior class of Columbia College in Washington, D.C.[557] He attended the University of Virginia, where he was a classmate of Edgar A. Poe and studied law under William Wirt.[558] From 1827 to 1828, Lee attended the Winchester Law School, which was open from 1824 to 1831.[559]

In the 1830s, Lee practiced law in Washington, D.C., being admitted as an attorney and counselor of the court on January 21, 1832.[560] By 1836, he was practicing law in Baltimore. Lee was also a renowned orator. That same year, he was selected to be the Fourth of July speaker in Alexandria, Virginia.[561] Lee was "cheerful and engaging, full of anecdote, which he ever told well."[562] In the November 1836 issue of the *Southern Literary Messenger*, Poe included a review of Lee's address that was delivered before the Baltimore Lyceum, Athenæum Society, William Wirt Society, Washington Lyceum, Philonomian Society and Franklin Association, Literary and Scientific Societies of Baltimore, on July 4, 1836. Poe wrote:

> *Having reason to be well aware of Mr. Lee's oratorical powers, we were not altogether at liberty to imagine his Address, merely from the deep attention with which, we are told, its delivery was received, the impassioned and scholar-like performance we now find it upon perusal. Few similar things indeed have afforded us any similar pleasure.*[563]

On June 15, 1837, he married Martha Ann Jenkins.[564] They would have three children: Richard Henry Lee (born on April 29, 1839), Mary Elizabeth Lee (born on November 5, 1840) and Mary Ida Lee (born in 1843), who sadly lived only six months.

Lee was considered someone who studied deeply in order to understand, and "he never designed to wound," so it should not have been a surprise to his peers that he would speak out against wrongdoing.[565] In October 1837, Lee as well as John Pendleton Kennedy were part of the Friends of Civil and Religious Liberty who gathered in Baltimore to express public opinion about "outrages committed at Boston upon the constitutional rights of adopted fellow citizens," referring to the Irish immigrants who had been attacked during the Broad Street Riot earlier that year.[566]

Lee was interested in a variety of subjects and continued to be an orator of choice. On June 6, 1839, Lee delivered an anniversary address before the

Horticultural Society of Maryland at its annual exhibition.[567] His speech before the American Colonization Society on the history of "The Star-Spangled Banner" was so popular that it was shared in the papers in 1843.[568]

From 1841 to 1845, and from 1850 to 1853, he served as the U.S. attorney for the District of Maryland. In 1855, he was appointed judge of the superior court of Baltimore. Lee continued being selected as the orator of various events, including the celebration of the landing of Pilgrims of Maryland in 1634.[569]

Z. Collins Lee was one of the few friends who "on the cold raw afternoon of October 9, 1849," attended Poe's funeral.[570] Poe was laid to rest near the grave of his grandfather in the small churchyard. In a letter, the funeral details were shared. "The body was followed to the grave by Mr. Herring, Dr. Snodgrass, Mr. Z. Collins Lee, (an old classmate) and myself. The service was performed by the Rev. Wm. T. D. Clemm, a son of James L. Clemm."[571]

Judge Z. Collins Lee lived only a decade beyond Poe. Lee gave seven lectures, with the last one the "Progress of the Age" given in January 1859 at the Maryland Institute.[572] Within the year, he died on November 26, 1859, after a sickness. He had expressed wanting to be buried beside his mother, and on November 29, 1859, he was buried in Congressional Cemetery, where "a large concourse of sorrowing friends united in the last solemnities."[573]

THE GRAVE

Z. Collins Lee's gravestone is a die in socket. The epitaph reads, "Sacred to the memory of Hon. Z. Collins Lee / Judge of the Superior Court of Baltimore City, Md. / Born Dec. 5, 1805 / Died Nov. 26, 1859.

GRAVE REFLECTIONS

Not far from Z. Collins Lee's grave is the monument for William Wirt (1772–1834) U.S. attorney general and author who had been offered a professorship of law at the University of Virginia while Poe was a student.[574] Poe respected Wirt's advice, writing, "From such a man as Mr. Wirt— the flattering character he has given of the work, will surely be to you a recommendation in its favor."[575] Poe's prose includes some gruesome tales that may have been taken from the headlines of his day. Truth is often stranger than fiction. In the case of William Wirt's grave, in 2003, the manager of

The grave of the Honorable Z. Collins Lee. *Author's collection.*

The grave of William Wirt in Congressional Cemetery. *Author's collection.*

Congressional Cemetery, Bill Fecke, received a series of odd phone calls asking about William Wirt's skull. The caller stated they had a collection of skulls, including that of William Wirt. Fecke decided that he should check Wirt's underground crypt, which is below a grand column. When he tried to enter, he could tell that the door was missing and the lock had been broken. Instead of a door, a large, heavy piece of granite closed the entrance to the tomb. A conservation task force was convened since Fecke was unable to access the tomb on his own. Once they were able to enter the tomb, they discovered that grave robbers had been there, but with several caskets in the crypt, they were unable to determine which grave belonged to Wirt. They then contacted a forensic anthropologist at the Smithsonian to look at a skull that D.C. council member Jim Graham had received from Allan Stypeck, a local bookstore owner who had been asked to appraise the collection of Robert L. White on his death in 2013. After much time and testing, it was determined that the discovered skull was that of William Wirt.[576] The skull has now been replaced into its tomb.

37

EDGAR ALLAN POE

(1809–1849)

WESTMINSTER BURYING GROUND, BALTIMORE, MARYLAND
NEAR FRONT GATE ON FAYETTE STREET
POET AND WRITER

*Generally, people praise extravagantly those of which I am ashamed,
and pass in silence what I fancy to be praise worthy.*[577]
—Poe

*I do not consider any one of my stories better than another.
There is a vast variety of kinds and, in degree of value, these kinds vary—but
each tale is equally good of its kind. The loftiest kind is that of the highest
imagination—and, for this reason only, "Ligeia" may be called my best tale.*[578]
—Poe

E.A. Poe must have always had a pen in hand. His mind buzzed with literary muses. His best work would be the next one he wrote. Could he imagine his words and his persona lasting for centuries?

LIFE BEFORE THE STONE

Edgar Poe was born in Boston to traveling actors David and Elizabeth *Arnold* Poe. Within a few years, he was orphaned when his father disappeared and his mother died.[579] In December 1811, Frances and John Allan, a wealthy couple from Richmond, Virginia, took in the young boy but never formally adopted him. In his youth, he was given the best education money could buy, and his foster mother adored him.[580] During his teen years, Poe began arguing with his foster father, who helped him be admitted to the University of Virginia.[581] He excelled in his studies but struggled financially, as he was not supplied with the proper funds for a university lifestyle. Poe turned to gambling, believing he could win enough to pay off his debts; he lost and owed even more money. Allan opposed gambling and was disappointed with Poe's behavior. Poe returned home, and his university school career ended. Allan put Poe to work, but longing for independence, Poe sought other employment and Allan denounced him as ungrateful.[582] Poe left the home of the Allans feeling like an outcast. He struggled financially.

In 1826, Poe enlisted in the U.S. Army using the name Edgar A. Perry. He published his first book, *Tamerlane and Other Poems*, the next year.[583] In 1829, his foster mother, Frances Allan, died and was buried before he could arrive home. Poe and Allan briefly reunited.[584] Poe published his second book, *Al Aaraaf, Tamerlane and Minor Poems*.[585] In 1830, John Allan married and began having sons with his second wife. Poe entered West Point, where he was court-martialed and dismissed from the military in early 1831.[586] That same year, his brother, Henry, died.[587] Poe continued writing and publishing his short stories in various papers. In 1833, he won a prize for "MS. Found in a Bottle."[588] In 1834, Allan died and left no inheritance for Poe. In 1835, Poe began working for the *Southern Literary Messenger*. He soon married his cousin Virginia in a formal ceremony on May 16, 1836.[589] He left the paper the next year to head to New York and then to Philadelphia. In 1839, he became the editor for *Gentleman's Magazine*. In 1841, he became the editor of *Graham's Magazine*. The next year, he met Charles Dickens during Dickens's tour of America.[590] In 1843, Poe hoped to secure a position as a clerk with the government, but this did not come to fruition.[591]

In 1844, the Poes moved to New York. In 1845, his famous poem "The Raven" was published in the *Evening Mirror*. That year, he became the editor of the *Broadway Journal*.[592] In 1846, the Poes moved to Fordham, New York, in hopes of Virginia's health improving. Virginia Poe died in January 1847. Although devasted, Poe continued to write. His poem *Eureka* was published in 1848. That year, he courted poet Sarah Helen Whitman. Within a short period, the engagement was called off due to Poe's drinking.[593] In the summer of 1849, Poe began a southern lecture tour to promote his proposed magazine *The Stylus*. He reconnected with his childhood sweetheart, Elmira *Royster* Shelton, and the two planned to marry.[594] In September 1849, he left Richmond for a trip north, where he stopped in Baltimore. He became quite ill, although the circumstances surrounding his death are shrouded in mystery. On October 7, 1849, Poe died in the Washington University Hospital. He was buried in his grandfather's lot at Westminster Burying Ground. Rufus Griswold wrote a malicious obituary. Poe's friends attempted to clear his name, but damage had already been done.[595]

THE GRAVE

Poe was originally buried in his grandfather's plot without a headstone, as it was damaged in the marble yard.[596] Schoolteacher Sara Sigourney Rice helped lead the effort to raise funds for a proper memorial for Poe's grave. Through the "pennies for Poe" drive, she and other teachers encouraged students to contribute coins.[597] Rice was also instrumental in contacting celebrity poets and writers to donate and attend the ceremony. In 1875, after a decade-long campaign, a monument was dedicated to Poe in a prominent part of the churchyard. Poignantly, Rice, who is buried in Mount Olivet Cemetery in Baltimore, has an unmarked grave.

Edgar Allan Poe's monument is a die, base and cap. The cap features decorative elements including a lyre and foliage above the base symbolizing the connection between heaven and earth. On the base of the marker there are floral accents above each epitaph. On the front of the monument is a portrait of Poe. The original bas-relief bust on the monument was carved of marble by Frederick Volck. This was replaced in 1938 by a bronze bust, which was replaced again in the 1970s after it was stolen. The original marble bust is in the Edgar Allan Poe House and Museum.[598] On the back of the monument is his epitaph that reads: "Edgar Allan Poe / Born / January 20, 1809 / Died / October 7, 1849." The birthdate should be January 19, 1809.

The grave of Edgar A. Poe. *Author's collection.*

Maria Clemm's remains were relocated to rest beside Poe.[599] Virginia Poe was reinterred by her husband a decade after the ceremony for the new monument. Their names were added to the monument in 1977.[600]

GRAVE REFLECTIONS

Early in this research project, I stumbled upon a newspaper article from New Year's Day 1847. The piece included an icon of a hand pointing toward a short blurb that reads, "Edgar A. Poe, the celebrated writer, and his lady, are both said to be dangerously ill, with the consumption, and in suffering circumstances."[601] It is easy to forget that Poe was a real person when there are so many stories about him wrapped in myth and legend. This newspaper clipping reminded me that he was a man who was sick along with his wife who would die within a month of the publication.

Taking this journey, and visiting Poe's grave numerous times, I was able to learn about him from so many different angles and perspectives. I admire his work ethic and his drive to make a living doing something for which he clearly had a talent. Writing was not pure joy for him. He did not always have an opportunity to advance southern literature or even American literature but frequently had to churn out popular stories that the newspaper readership demanded.

The amazing part of this project was that by connecting with Poe through his friends, family and foes, I was able to have a deeper connection to his work, to literature and to sacred burial grounds. Visiting the graves transformed me. I took my own whiff of orris root at the grave of Frances Allan; I sat by the water near where Susan Ingram gathered with family and friends 173 years ago when Poe read poetry to them. Although we do not have recordings of Poe reading his work, Dean Knight from the Poe Museum in Richmond offers several great renditions online, including "Ulalume," which seemed magical to Ingram.[602] While I learned much about Poe during this project, I also learned about poets and writers I had not previously studied, including Philip Pendleton Cooke of Winchester, Virginia. Poe delighted in his work and valued his opinion, so it was Poe who introduced me to Cooke and his beautiful poetry. I read Cooke's poetry at his grave. In 2022, Poe Baltimore hosted monthly events, both online and in person, that celebrated Virginia Poe. In August, just two days before the bicentennial of her birth, I attended their gothic tea party and reception at Westminster Hall and Burying Ground.[603] These are the very events that I dreamed of attending when I was a teen being handed newspaper clippings about Poe and his burial place. I am so grateful to the newspaper readers, historians and scholars who have made this all possible.

NOTES

Introduction

1. "The Letters of Edgar Allan Poe," Edgar Allan Poe Society of Baltimore, https://www.eapoe.org/ [hereafter EAPS].
2. C. Young and D. Light, "Interrogating Spaces of and for the Dead as 'Alternative Space': Cemeteries, Corpses and Sites of Dark Tourism," *International Review of Social Research* 6, no. 2 (2016): 61–72.
3. "Blandford Cemetery," *Encyclopedia of Virginia*, https://encyclopediavirginia.org/2990hpr-98ebb609681a271/.
4. "National Register Information System," National Register of Historic Places, National Park Service, October 15, 1992.
5. "Bruton Parish Churchyard: A Self-Guided Tour," Bruton Parish Church, https://www.brutonparish.org/history.
6. Cave Hill Cemetery, https://www.cavehillcemetery.com/.
7. Emily Robinson, "Poe's Washington Excursion," *Boundary Stones: WETA's Washington DC History Blog*, October 30, 2017, https://boundarystones.weta.org/2017/10/30/poes-washington-excursion.
8. Congressional Cemetery, https://congressionalcemetery.org/.
9. Green Mount Cemetery, https://www.greenmountcemetery.com/.
10. "Elijah Bond Memorial Gravestone," Talking Board Historical Society, https://tbhs.org/elijah-bond-memorial-gravestone/.
11. Edwin Slipek Jr., "Digging Up Bones," *Style Weekly*, August 9, 2019, https://www.styleweekly.com/richmond/digging-up-bones/.
12. "Hollywood Cemetery," *Cultural Landscape Foundation*, https://tclf.org/landscapes/hollywood-cemetery.

13. The two other cemeteries with two U.S. presidents include Arlington National Cemetery, where John F. Kennedy and William Howard Taft are buried, and United First Parish in Quincy, Massachusetts, where John Adams and John Quincy Adams are buried.

14. Loudon Park Cemetery, https://loudon-park.com/.

15. "Lexington City Council Votes to Rename Stonewall Jackson Memorial Cemetery," WFXR Newsroom, July 7, 2020.

16. "Executive Papers of Governor James McDowell," Library of Virginia, https://ead.lib.virginia.edu/.

17. T. Tyler Potterfield, *Nonesuch Place: A History of the Richmond Landscape* (Charleston, SC: The History Press, 2009), 88.

18. Christopher P. Semtner, *The Poe Shrine: Building the World's Finest Edgar Allan Poe Collection* (Charleston, SC: Arcadia Publishing, 2017), 29–30.

19. Fancy Me Mad Tales from Beyond the Grave tour brochure, 2017.

20. Historic St. Johns Church website FAQ, https://www.historicstjohnschurch.org.

21. Alyson L. Taylor-White, *Shockoe Hill Cemetery: A Richmond Landmark History* (Charleston, SC: The History Press, 2017), 12.

22. David Maurer, "Set in Stone: The Serenity of UVA's Cemetery Belies a Colorful Past," *Virginia Magazine*, UVA Alumni Association, https://uvamagazine.org/articles/set_in_stone; *Richmond Enquirer*, April 21, 1846, 4.

23. *Richmond Enquirer*, May 26, 1846, 4.

24. "Poe as a Student," *Raven Society*, https://aig.alumni.virginia.edu/raven/poe-resources/poe-as-a-student.

25. Edgar Allan Poe, "Spirits of the Dead," in *Al Aaraaf, Tamerlane and Minor Poems* (Baltimore: Hatch & Dunning, 1829), 65–66.

1. Elizabeth Arnold Hopkins Poe

26. Geddeth Smith, *The Brief Career of Eliza Poe* (Granbury, NJ: Fairleigh Dickinson University Press, 1988), 45.

27. Arthur Hobson Quinn, *Edgar Allan Poe: A Critical Biography* (New York: D. Appleton-Century, 1941), 41.

28. Smith, *Brief Career of Eliza Poe*, 44.

29. Ibid., 81.

30. Jeffrey Meyers, *Edgar Allan Poe: His Life and Legacy* (New York City: Cooper Square Press, 1992), 3.

31. Quinn, *Edgar Allan Poe*, 24.

32. Smith, *Brief Career of Eliza Poe*, 100.

33. Ibid., 82.

34. Charles Marshall Graves, "Landmarks of Poe in His Loved City," *Times Dispatch* (Richmond, VA), February 19, 1905, 5.

35. Smith, *Brief Career of Eliza Poe*, 118.
36. Quinn, *Edgar Allan Poe*, 40.
37. Smith, *Brief Career of Eliza Poe*, 129.
38. Quinn, *Edgar Allan Poe*, 45–46.
39. Dwight R. Thomas and David K. Jackson, *The Poe Log: A Documentary Life of Edgar Allan Poe 1809–1849* (Boston: G.K. Hall, 1987), 14.
40. Written on a watercolor painting by Elizabeth Poe in 1808 and gifted to her son on her deathbed.
41. Semtner writes that it was Mackenize in *Poe Shrine*, 29, while Bob Hufford, reenactor at St. John's Church stated that it was Allan.
42. According to Bob Hufford, reenactor at St. John's Church.
43. *Times Dispatch*, March 10, 1912, 37.
44. *Times Dispatch*, April 11, 1928, 2.
45. *Times Dispatch*, April 11, 1928, 2.
46. *Times Dispatch*, April 11, 1928, 1.

2. Frances Keeling Valentine Allan

47. Kim Bridges, "The Valentine Richmond History Center," *Richmond Family Magazine*, May 24, 2012, richmondfamilymagazine.com.
48. "To Fanny," Poe Museum, June 10, 2015, https://poemuseum.org/to-fanny/.
49. Christopher P. Semtner, *Edgar Allan Poe's Richmond: Raven in the River City* (Charleston, SC: Arcadia Publishing, 2012), 23.
50. "Allen, John, m. Fanny Valentine, in Richmond (CC.Feb.26,1803)," in Index of Marriages in Massachusetts Centinel and Columbian Centinel 1784 to 1840, 55.
51. "To Fanny."
52. Semtner, *Edgar Allan Poe's Richmond*, 24–25.
53. Thomas and Jackson, *Poe Log*.
54. Semtner, *Edgar Allan Poe's Richmond*, 24.
55. Brendan Wolfe, "Fire, Richmond Theatre (1811)," *Encyclopedia Virginia*, December 14, 2021, https://encyclopediavirginia.org/entries/fire-richmond-theatre-1811.
56. Ibid.
57. Semtner, *Edgar Allan Poe's Richmond*, 26.
58. "Monumental Church," National Park Service, National Historic Landmark summary listing.
59. Keshia A. Case and Christopher P. Semtner, *Edgar Allan Poe in Richmond* (Charleston, SC: Arcadia Publishing, 2009), 16.
60. "Frances Allan," Edgar Allan Poe National Historic Site, October 15, 1818, https://www.nps.gov/people/poe-francesallan.htm.
61. Ibid.
62. Edgar Allan Poe to John Allan, January 3, 1831, EAPS.

63. "Was a Friend of Poe: Miss Ingram Tells of Poet's Gift of a Copy of Ulalume," *Baltimore Sun*, February 26, 1905, 13.

64. Ibid.

65. April Long, "How the Humble Iris Root Became One of the Most Prized—and Pricey—Fragrance Ingredients on the Planet," *Town & Country*, August 26, 2021, https://www.townandcountrymag.com/style/beauty-products/a37273674/orris-perfume-iris/.

66. Edgar Allan Poe to John Allan, January 3, 1831, EAPS.

67. Christopher P. Semtner, *Haunting Poe: His Afterlife in Richmond & Beyond* (Charleston, SC: The History Press, 2022), 41.

3. John Allan

68. Poe to John Allan, October 16, 1831.

69. Semtner, *Edgar Allan Poe's Richmond*, 23.

70. Ibid., 24–25.

71. "Allen, John, m. Fanny Valentine, in Richmond (CC.Feb.26,1803)," 55.

72. "To Fanny."

73. Thomas and Jackson, *Poe Log*.

74. Semtner, *Edgar Allan Poe's Richmond*, 24.

75. Ibid., 16.

76. Semtner writes that it was Mackenize in *Poe Shrine*, 29, while Bob Hufford, reenactor at St. John's Church, stated that it was Allan.

77. Letters from John Allan dated March 21, 1818; June 22, 1818; and November 27, 1819.

78. October 30, 1815 letter from John Allan to Charles Ellis regarding Poe's reading, and November 27, 1819 letter from John Allan to William Galt regarding Poe being a good scholar.

79. John Allan to Poe, June 22, 1818.

80. John Allan to George Dubourg, August 14, 1817.

81. John Allan to Poe, January 23, 1816; July 17, 1816; December 7, 1816; April 18, 1820; April 23, 1823.

82. Mary E. Phillips, "Section 02," in *Edgar Allan Poe: The Man* (Chicago: John C. Winston Company, 1926), 165.

83. Eugene L. Didier, *Life of Edgar A. Poe* (New York: W.J. Widdleton, 1877), 31.

84. John Allan to Henry Poe, November 1, 1824.

85. *Richmond Compiler*, January 5, 1825.

86. "Poe as a Student."

87. Edgar Allan Poe to John Allan, May 25, 1826.

88. "Virginia Landmarks Register," Virginia Department of Historic Resources, https://www.dhr.virginia.gov/historic-registers/002-5055/.

89. Edgar Allan Poe to John Allan, May 25, 1826.

90. Edgar Allan Poe to John Allan, March 19, 1827.

91. "Poe as a Student."

92. Edgar Allan Poe to John Allan, March 19, 1827.

93. Edgar Allan Poe to John Allan, January 3, 1831.

94. Edgar Allan Poe to John Allan, April 12, 1833.

95. Semtner, *Edgar Allan Poe's Richmond*, 61.

96. Charles Slack, "Promoting Poe: Four Cities Lay Claim to Nation's Dark Genius," *Richmond Times Dispatch*, February 9, 1992, 3.

4. Anne Moore Valentine

97. Edgar Allan Poe, "Alone," *Scribner's Monthly*, September 1875.

98. Kenneth Silverman, *Edgar A. Poe, A Biography: Mournful and Never-ending Remembrance* (New York: Harper Perennial, 1991), 14. Silverman lists her as the "older sister," but personal correspondence with Chris Semtner, curator of the Poe Museum on August 25, 2022, notes that she would be "one or two years younger than her sister Frances."

99. "To Fanny."

100. Semtner, *Edgar Allan Poe's Richmond*, 23.

101. John Allan to Charles Ellis, June 23, 1818.

102. "Died," *Daily Richmond Times*, January 26, 1850.

5. Edward Valentine

103. Poe to Edward Valentine, November 20, 1848.

104. *Catalogue of Washington College* (Lexington, VA: Trustees and Alumni, 1852), 17.

105. Semtner, *Edgar Allan Poe's Richmond*, 30.

106. Botetourt County Deed Book 31, 182–184, notation from EAPS, https://www.eapoe.org/works/letters/p4811200.htm.

107. Census Year: 1860; Botetourt, Virginia; Archive Collection Number: T1132; Roll: 5; Page: 21; Line: 34; Agriculture.

108. "Historic Avenel," *Living in the Heart of Virginia-LHOV*, June 16, 2020, television show. During the segment, Irene Catlin, Historic Avenel facility director, discusses the history and the possibility of ghosts.

109. Sir Walter Scott, *The Monastery: A Romance. By the Author of "Waverley" Sir Walter Scott* (Edinburgh: Longman, Hurst, Rees, Orme and Brown, 1820).

110. Jessie Pounds, "'Ghost' of Poe Appears at Historic Haunt Avenel," *News & Advance*, February 18, 2013, https://newsadvance.com/news/local/ghost-of-poe-appears-at-historic-haunt-avenel/article_54dee6dd-   c123-5c2a-8431-f9bfbb1a54b1.html.

6. William Galt

111. Edgar Allan Poe, *The Gold-Bug* (Boston: D. Estes & Company, 1899), 61.
112. G. Melvin Herndon, "From Scottish Orphan to Virginia Planter: William Galt, Jr. 1801–1851," *Virginia Magazine of History and Biography* 87, no. 3 (July 1979): 326.
113. Semtner, *Edgar Allan Poe's Richmond*, 23.
114. Herndon, "From Scottish Orphan to Virginia Planter," 327.
115. Ibid., 331.
116. Ibid., 326.

7. William Henry Leonard Poe

117. October–November 1829 letter from Poe to John Neal, EAPS.
118. February 8, 1813 letter from aunt, Eliza Poe to Frances Allan, Ellis and Allan correspondence in the Library of Congress, quoted in Hervey Allan and Thomas Olive Mabbott, *Poe's Brother: The Poems of William Henry Leonard Poe* (New York: George H. Doran Company, 1926), 20.
119. David Arkell, "Poe in England," *PN Review* 19, no. 3 (January 1993): 7.
120. Silverman, *Edgar A. Poe*, 30.
121. Ibid.
122. Hervey Allen, *Israfel: The Life and Times of Edgar Allan Poe* (New York: George H. Doran Company, 1926), 142.
123. Silverman, *Edgar A. Poe*, 82–83, 125.
124. Ibid., 85.

8. David Poe Sr.

125. Edgar Allan Poe, "Memorandum [Autobiographical Note]," manuscript, May 29, 1841, EAPS.
126. Birth years are listed as 1742 or 1743. I follow the one noted on the grave since sources differ.
127. "Edgar Allan Poe in Baltimore," EAPS.
128. Poe Museum, "Poe and Independence Day," July 4, 2014, https://poemuseum.org/poe-and-independence-day/.
129. "Chronology of Poe in Baltimore," EAPS.
130. Ibid.
131. Ibid.
132. Ibid.
133. Poe Baltimore, "Meet Virginia: A Death Day Commemoration," YouTube, January 30, 2022, timestamp 12:22, https://www.youtube.com/watch?v=SGbXTXzWyws&t=121s.

9. Robert Craig Stanard

134. Edgar Allan Poe, "Marginalia [part XV]," *Southern Literary Messenger* 15, no. 6 (June 1849): 336.
135. Semtner, *Edgar Allan Poe's Richmond*, 40.
136. Ibid., 42.
137. Ibid., 36–38.
138. Ibid., 38.
139. Ibid., 78.
140. Ibid., 95.
141. Weekly Raleigh (NC) Register, June 10, 1857, 3.
142. Ashley Whitehead Luskey, "'A Debt of Honor': Elite Women's Rituals of Cultural Authority in the Confederate Capital" (graduate dissertation at West Virginia University, 2014), 64–65.
143. John S. Patton, "Biography," in *Poems of John R. Thompson* (New York: Charles Scribner's Sons, 1920), xix.

10. Jane Stith Craig Stanard

144. Edgar Allan Poe, "To Helen," (1831).
145. Edwin Slipek, "Adam Craig House," Architecture Richmond, August 3, 2017, https://architecturerichmond.com/inventory/adam-craig-house/.
146. *Virginia Argus*, May 13, 1808; *William and Mary Quarterly* 11, no. 2 (April 1931): 159.
147. Semtner, *Edgar Allan Poe's Richmond*, 40.
148. October 18, 1848 letter from Poe to Sarah Helen Whitman.
149. March 10, 1859 letter from Maria Clemm to Sarah Helen Whitman.
150. Semtner, *Edgar Allan Poe's Richmond*, 43.
151. Ibid.
152. Sarah Helen Whitman, *Edgar Poe and His Critics* (New York: Rudd & Carleton, 1860), 49.
153. Semtner, *Edgar Allan Poe's Richmond*, 43.
154. Stanard's epitaph notes she died at thirty-one, although based on her birth records, she would have been closer to thirty-three.
155. Poe's poem "The Valley Nis," published in 1831, evolved into "The Valley of Unrest."
156. Taylor-White, *Shockoe Hill Cemetery*, 107.

11. Robert Matthew Sully

157. Edgar Allan Poe, "The Oval Portrait," *Broadway Journal* 1, no. 17 (April 1845): 264–65.

158. Charles E. Hatch Jr., "Robert Sully at Jamestown, 1854," *William and Mary Quarterly* 22, no. 4 (October 1942): 343.

159. Carrie Rebora Barratt, "Thomas Sully (1783–1872) and Queen Victoria," in *Heilbrunn Timeline of Art History* (New York: Metropolitan Museum of Art, 2000), http://www.metmuseum.org/toah/hd/tsly/hd_tsly.htm.

160. Semtner, *Edgar Allan Poe's Richmond*, 16.

161. Hatch, "Robert Sully at Jamestown," 344.

162. Ibid.

163. Case and Semtner, *Edgar Allan Poe in Richmond*, 69.

164. Jordan R. Dodd, *Early American Marriages: Virginia to 1850* (Bountiful, UT: Precision Indexing Publishers, 1999).

165. Michael J. Deas, "Portraits by Robert M. Sully," in *The Portraits and Daguerreotypes of Edgar Allan Poe* (Charlottesville: University Press of Virginia, 1989), 144.

166. Semtner, *Edgar Allan Poe's Richmond*, 78.

167. "Two Poe Portraits," Alumni Bulletin of the University of Virginia 12–13 (1919): 106.

168. The letter from Landon C. Bell in "Two Poe Portraits" reads that Poe saw the painting before his death and "was very much pleased with it," while Deas, "Portraits by Robert M. Sully," 143, notes, "Poe would not live to see the painting completed."

169. Semtner, *Edgar Allan Poe's Richmond*, 95.

170. Deas, "Portraits by Robert M. Sully," 144.

171. Hatch, "Robert Sully at Jamestown," 346.

172. "Two Poe Portraits," 107.

173. "Died," *Daily Dispatch* (Richmond, VA), November 13, 1855.

174. "Two Poe Portraits," 107.

175. Sully's death date is reported as October 16, 28 and 30 in various sources.

12. Nathaniel Beverly Tucker

176. Poe to Nathaniel Beverley Tucker, December 1, 1835.

177. Robert Doares, "The Life and Literature of Nathaniel Beverley Tucker," *Colonial Williamsburg Journal*, Autumn 2001, https://research.colonialwilliamsburg.org/Foundation/journal/Autumn01/tucker.cfm.

178. Ibid.

179. Ibid.

180. Ibid.

181. Poe to Nathaniel Beverly Tucker, December 1, 1835.

182. Poe's review of George Balcombe, *Southern Literary Messenger* 3, no. 1 (January 1837): 49–58.

183. Doares, "Life and Literature of Nathaniel Beverley Tucker."

13. William Wertenbaker

184. Edgar Allan Poe, "The Imp of the Perverse," 1850.

185. *Jeffersonian Republican* (Charlottesville, VA), April 12, 1882, available through *Virginia Chronicle*, Library of Virginia, https://virginiachronicle.com/.

186. *Jeffersonian Republican*.

187. Douglass Sherley, "Mr. William Wertenbaker—His Golden Wedding," *Virginia University Magazine* 19, no. 1 (October 1879): 42–43.

188. *Jeffersonian Republican*.

189. National Archives, "From Thomas Jefferson to William Wertenbaker, 30 January 1826," *Founders Online*, https://founders.archives.gov/documents/Jefferson/98-01-02-5868.

190. *Jeffersonian Republican*.

191. "Poe as a Student."

192. William Wertenbaker, "Edgar A. Poe," *Virginia University Magazine*, November–December 1868.

193. Ibid., 115.

194. Ibid.

195. "Poe as a Student."

196. "Catalogue of the Library of the University of Virginia," University of Virginia Library Online Exhibits, June 16, 2022, https://explore.lib.virginia.edu/items/show/2083.

197. *Jeffersonian Republican*.

198. *Jeffersonian Republican*.

199. *Jeffersonian Republican*.

200. Wertenbaker, "Edgar A. Poe," 114–17.

201. Sherley, "Mr. William Wertenbaker," 43.

202. *Jeffersonian Republican*.

203. George Tucker, "A Discourse on the Progress of Philosophy, and Its Influence on the Intellect and Moral Character of Man; delivered before the Virginia Historical and Philosophical Society, February 5, 1835. By George Tucker, Professor of Moral Philosophy in the University of Virginia," *Southern Literary Messenger* 1 (April 1835): 405–21.

204. Quoted in Michael Dirda, "To Understand Ourselves," *Johns Hopkins Magazine*, August 2009, https://magazine.jhu.edu/2009/08/27/to-understand-ourselves/.

14. John T.L. Preston

205. Edgar Allan Poe, "The System of Doctor Tarr and Professor Fether," *Graham's Magazine*, November 1845.

206. Colonel J.T.L. Preston, "Some Reminiscences of Edgar A. Poe as a Schoolboy," in Sara Sigourney Rice's *Edgar Allan Poe: A Memorial Volume* (Baltimore: Turnbull Brothers, 1877), 37.

207. Ibid., 40.

208. Ibid., 41–42.

209. Rod Andrew Jr., *Long Gray Lines: The Southern Military School Tradition, 1839–1915* (Chapel Hill, NC: University of North Carolina Press, 2001), 12.

210. The National Cyclopaedia of American Biography (New York: J.T. White, 1967), 245.

211. *Evening Star* (Washington, D.C.), March 14, 1857.

212. *Southern Presbyterian Review*, vol. 16 (Charleston, SC: Southern Presbyterian Review, 1866), 89.

213. Henry A. Wise, *Drawing Out the Man: The VMI Story* (Lexington, VA: VMI Alumni Association, 1978), 64.

214. The inscription *Laus Deo* is Latin for "praise to God."

215. "Margaret J. Preston," *Knoxville (TN) Tribune*, March 29, 1897.

216. Memorial Edition Poems and Essay of Edgar Allan Poe (New York: W.J. Widdleton, 1876), cxxxvi.

15. John Collins McCabe

217. March 3, 1836 letter from Poe to John Collins McCabe.

218. John Collins McCabe, *Scraps* (Richmond, VA: J.C. Walker, 1835).

219. *Richmond (VA) Whig*, July 25, 1837.

220. March 3, 1836 letter from Poe to John Collins McCabe.

221. Middletown (DE) Transcript, April 11, 1868.

222. Edgar Allan Poe, "A Chapter on Autography," *Graham's Magazine*, December 1841.

223. Virginia, Marriage Registers, 1853–1935, Library of Virginia, Richmond, Virginia.

224. "Married," *Middletown (DE) Transcript*, September 19, 1868.

225. "Clinton McCabe," *Cecil Whig* (Elkton, MD) July 15, 1916, 1; 1870 United States Census, New Castle, Delaware, Appoquinimink Hundred line 24.

16. Rosalie Mackenzie Poe

226. Poe to William Poe, August 20, 1835.

227. John Allan to Henry Poe, November 1, 1824.

228. Semtner, *Edgar Allan Poe's Richmond*, 16.

229. Silverman, *Edgar A. Poe*, 25.

230. Wolfe, "Fire, Richmond Theatre (1811)."

231. Semtner, *Edgar Allan Poe's Richmond*, 26.

232. Silverman, *Edgar A. Poe*, 25.

233. Ibid., 125.

234. Susan Archer Weiss, "The Sister of Edgar A. Poe," *Continent* 3, no. 6 (June 1883): 817.

235. Silverman, *Edgar A. Poe*, 125.

236. Ibid., 303–4.

237. Ibid., 423.

238. Semtner, *Edgar Allan Poe's Richmond*, 93.

239. Ibid., 95–96.

240. Silverman, *Edgar A. Poe*, 426.

241. Weiss, "Sister of Edgar A. Poe," 817.

242. Ibid., 818.

243. Ibid.

244. Semtner, *Edgar Allan Poe's Richmond*, 113.

245. Silverman, *Edgar A. Poe*, 441.

246. Ibid., 442.

247. "Danville Cemeteries," City of Danville, Virginia, https://www.danville-va.gov/571/Cemeteries.

248. Semtner, *Edgar Allan Poe's Richmond*, 112.

17. John Pendleton Kennedy

249. Poe to John P. Kennedy, December 31, 1840.

250. Kennedy to Poe, September 19, 1835.

251. Library of Congress, "Kennedy, John Pendleton 1795–1870," *Biographical Directory of the United States Congress*, https://bioguide.congress.gov/search/bio/K000109.

252. John Earle Uhler, "The Delphian Club: A Contribution to the Literary History of Baltimore in the Early Nineteenth Century," *Maryland Historical Magazine*, December 1925.

253. Library of Congress, "Kennedy, John Pendleton 1795–1870."

254. Jeffrey A. Savoye, "Poe and Baltimore: Crossroads and Redemption," in *Poe and Place*, ed. Philip Edward Philips (Cham, CH: Palgrave Macmillan, 2018), 109.

255. Kennedy to George W. Fahnestock, April 13, 1869, in John Earle Uhler "Kennedy's Novels and His Posthumous Works," *American Literature* 3, no. 4 (January 1932): 222.

256. Silverman, *Edgar A. Poe*, 101.

257. Poe to Kennedy, March 15, 1835.

258. William Doyle Hull II, "Part I, Chapter I," in *A Canon of the Critical Works of Edgar Allan Poe* (Charlottesville: University of Virginia, 1941), 39.

259. Library of Congress, "Kennedy, John Pendleton 1795–1870."

260. Kennedy to Poe, December 1, 1845.

261. Library of Congress, "Kennedy, John Pendleton 1795–1870."

262. Ibid.

263. David O. Tomlinson, "John Pendleton Kennedy: An Essay in Bibliography," *Resources for American Literary Study* 9, no. 2 (Fall 1979): 142–43.

18. Philip Pendleton Cooke

264. Poe to Philip P. Cooke, August 9, 1846.

265. Kevin J. Hayes, "The Literary Professional and the Country Gentleman: The Letters of Edgar Allan Poe and Philip Pendleton Cooke," in *The Edinburg Companion to Nineteenth-Century American Letters and Letter-Writing*, eds. Celeste-Marie Bernier, Judie Newman and Matthew Pethers (Edinburgh: Edinburgh University Press, 2016), 555.

266. William Whitley, "Philip Pendleton Cooke (1816–1850)," *Encyclopedia Virginia*, December 22, 2021, https://encyclopediavirginia.org/entries/cooke-philip-pendleton-1816-1850.

267. Hayes, "Literary Professional and the Country Gentleman," 555.

268. Ibid., 556.

269. Ibid.

270. Poe to Nathaniel Beverly Tucker, December 1, 1835.

271. Poe to Philip P. Cooke, August 4, 1846.

272. Whitley, "Philip Pendleton Cooke (1816–1850)."

273. Hayes, "Literary Professional and the Country Gentleman," 556.

274. Whitley, "Philip Pendleton Cooke (1816–1850)."

275. Cooke to John R. Thompson, October 23, 1849.

276. Ibid.

19. Amasa Converse

277. Edgar Allan Poe, *Eureka* (Wiley & Putnam, 1848).

278. L.P. Yandell, *A Biographical Sketch of the Late Amasa Converse, D.D.* (Louisville, KY: Presbytery of Louisville, 1873), 4.

279. Ibid., 5.

280. Ibid., 6.

281. Ibid., 7.

282. Ibid., 9.

283. "Church Paper Story Is Told," *Charlotte (NC) Observer*, March 16, 1947, 53.

284. Yandell, *Biographical Sketch*, 9.

285. Paul D. Converse, "Richmond Family Lived Well on Little Old Records Show Changes in Costs of Food," *Richmond (VA) Times Dispatch*, April 16, 1950.

286. Semtner, *Edgar Allan Poe's Richmond*, 78; "Today Marks Edgar Poe's 177th Wedding Anniversary," Poe Museum, May 16, 2013, https://poemuseum.org/today-marks-edgar-poes-177th-wedding-anniversary/.

287. Semtner, *Edgar Allan Poe's Richmond*, 78.

288. Susan Archer Weiss, *The Home Life of Poe* (New York: Broadway Publishing Company, 1907), 80.

289. Yandell, *Biographical Sketch*, 10–11.

290. Ibid., 12.

291. Ibid., 13.

292. Ibid., 14.

293. "Church Paper Story Is Told," *Charlotte (NC) Observer*, March 16, 1947.

294. Yandell, *Biographical Sketch*, 14.

295. Ibid., 15.

20. Maria Poe Clemm

296. Poe to William Poe, August 20, 1835.

297. Marie Louise Shew to John Henry Ingram, March 28, 1875.

298. "Chronology of Poe in Baltimore," EAPS.

299. Ibid.

300. Ibid.

301. Silverman, *Edgar A. Poe*, 81.

302. Ibid.

303. Ibid.

304. "Chronology of Poe in Baltimore," EAPS.

305. Silverman, *Edgar A. Poe*, 323.

306. Ibid., 104.

307. Weiss, *Home Life of Poe*, 77.

308. Poe to Maria Clemm, August 29, 1835.

309. Semtner, *Edgar Allan Poe's Richmond*, 78.

310. Poe to Maria Clemm, April 7, 1844.

311. *Alton (IL) Telegraph and Democratic Review*, January 1, 1847.

312. Silverman, *Edgar A. Poe*, 420.

313. Poe to Maria Clemm, December 23, 1848.

314. Poe to Maria Clemm, July 14, 1849, near Richmond letter.

315. Poe to Maria Clemm, July 14, 1849, Richmond Saturday night letter.

316. Poe to Maria Clemm, July 19, 1849.

317. Poe to Maria Clemm, August 29, 1849.

318. Poe to Maria Clemm, September 18, 1849.

319. Poe to Maria Clemm, September 18, 1849.

320. "Mrs. Maria Clemm," EAPS.

321. Ibid.
322. Silverman, *Edgar A. Poe*, 439.
323. Ibid., 440.
324. Ibid., 439.
325. "Mrs. Maria Clemm," EAPS.
326. "Mrs. Maria Clemm," *The Conservative* (McConnelsville, OH), March 31, 1871.
327. "The Poet Edgar Allan Poe Dedication of a Monument to His Memory," *Baltimore Sun*, November 18, 1875.
328. "A Monument to the Memory of Edgar Allan Poe," history marker at Westminster Burying Ground.
329. Maria Clemm to Nancy Richmond, February 25, 1859, in Silverman, *Edgar A. Poe*, 447.

21. Virginia Eliza Clemm Poe

330. Poe to Virginia Poe, June 12, 1846.
331. Edgar Allan Poe, "The Philosophy of Composition," *Graham's Magazine*, April 1846.
332. Silverman, *Edgar A. Poe*, 81.
333. Ibid., 81.
334. "Chronology of Poe in Baltimore," EAPS.
335. Silverman, *Edgar A. Poe*, 323.
336. Ibid., 104.
337. August 29, 1835 letter from Poe to Maria Clemm.
338. See Nicholas L. Syrett, *American Child Bridge: A History of Minors and Marriage in the United States* (Chapel Hill: University of North Carolina Press, 2016).
339. Weiss, *Home Life of Poe*, 75.
340. *Poe Baltimore*, "Meet Virginia: A Death Day Commemoration," YouTube, January 30, 2022, timestamp 5:14, https://www.youtube.com/watch?v=SGbXTXzWyws&t=121s; Weiss, *Home Life of Poe*, 77.
341. Meyers, *Edgar Allan Poe*, 85.
342. Weiss, *Home Life of Poe*, 80.
343. Jeffrey Abugel, *Edgar Allan Poe's Petersburg: The Untold Story of the Raven in the Cockade City* (Charleston, SC: The History Press, 2013), 101.
344. Lucinda Hawksley, "The Mysterious Tale of Charles Dickens's Raven," BBC, August 20, 2015, https://www.bbc.com/culture/article/20150820-the-mysterious-tale-of-charles-dickenss-raven.
345. Weiss, *Home Life of Poe*, 102.
346. Ibid., 103.
347. Silverman, *Edgar A. Poe*, 287.
348. Ibid., 289.
349. Ibid., 290.

350. Virginia Clemm Poe, "[Valentine to Edgar Allan Poe]," manuscript, February 14, 1846, EAPS.

351. Poe to George W. Eveleth, January 4, 1848.

352. Ibid.

353. Silverman, *Edgar A. Poe*, 302.

354. *Alton (IL) Telegraph and Democratic Review*, January 1, 1847, 2.

355. "Meet Virginia," timestamp 10:24.

356. "Mrs. Virginia Clemm Poe," EAPS.

357. "The Poet Edgar Allan Poe Dedication of a Monument to His Memory," *Baltimore Sun*, November 18, 1875, 1.

358. "A Monument to the Memory of Edgar Allan Poe," history marker at Westminster Burying Ground.

359. John C. Miller, "The Exhumations and Reburials of Edgar and Virginia Poe and Mrs. Clemm," *Poe Studies* 7, no. 2 (December 1974): 46–47.

22. Hiram Haines

360. Poe to Hiram Haines, August 19, 1836.

361. Abugel, *Edgar Allan Poe's Petersburg*, 57.

362. Ibid., 56.

363. Ibid., 59–60.

364. Ibid., 63.

365. Ibid., 68.

366. Ibid., 57.

367. See Abugel, *Edgar Allan Poe's Petersburg*.

368. Abugel, *Edgar Allan Poe's Petersburg*, 68.

369. Ibid., 71.

370. Ibid., 70.

371. Ibid., 101.

372. Ibid.

373. Ibid., 105.

374. Ibid., 111.

375. Poe to Hiram Haines, April 24, 1840.

376. Ibid.

377. "Death of Hiram Haines, Esq.," *Richmond (VA) Enquirer*, January 9, 1841.

378. Edward Young, *The Poetical Works of Edward Young with Life* (London: Gall & Inglis, 1870), 39.

23. Thomas Willis White

379. Christopher P. Semtner, "Poe in Richmond: The New Face of Thomas Willis White," *Edgar Allan Poe Review* 18, no. 1 (Spring 2017): 78.

380. Paul Ashdown, "White, Thomas Willis (28 March 1788–19 January 1843)," in *American National Biography* (Oxford University Press, 1999), https://doi.org/10.1093/anb/9780198606697.article.1601755.

381. "Death of Mrs. Bernard," *Weekly Star* (Wilmington, NC), April 30, 1897.

382. The inscription on Thomas Henry White's marker reads he died "of the prevailing Epidemic." An article in the *Richmond (VA) Enquirer*, October 9, 1832, points to a cholera outbreak in various cities.

383. "Death of Mrs. Bernard."

384. *Southern Literary Messenger* 1, no. 7 (March 1835): 333–36.

385. Ibid., 336.

386. *Southern Literary Messenger* 1, no. 8 (April 1835): 448–50.

387. Edgar Allan Poe to Thomas W. White, April 30, 1835.

388. Ibid.

389. Ashdown, "White, Thomas Willis."

390. Thomas W. White to Edgar Allan Poe, September 29, 1835.

391. "Married," *Fayetteville (NC) Weekly Observer*, January 21, 1836.

392. *Southern Literary Messenger* 9, no. 2 (February 1843): 1.

393. Sara B. Bearss, "John Woodburn Davies (1818–1883)," *Dictionary of Virginia Biography*, Library of Virginia, http://www.lva.virginia.gov/public/dvb/bio.asp?b=Davies_John_Woodburn.

24. Eliza White

394. Edgar Allan Poe, "Lines Written in an Album," *Southern Literary Messenger* 1 (September 1835): 748.

395. The inscription on Thomas Henry White's marker reads he died "of the prevailing Epidemic." An article in the *Richmond (VA) Enquirer*, October 9, 1832, points to a cholera outbreak in various cities.

396. "Death of Mrs. Bernard," *Weekly Star* (Wilmington, NC), April 30, 1897.

397. "Death of Mrs. Bernard"; Semtner, "Poe in Richmond," 81.

398. "Today Marks Edgar Poe's 177th Wedding Anniversary," Poe Museum, May 16, 2013, https://poemuseum.org/today-marks-edgar-poes-177th-wedding-anniversary/.

399. "Death of Mrs. Bernard."

400. Semtner, "Poe in Richmond," 81.

25. Elizabeth Van Lew

401. Edgar Allan Poe, "The Spectacles," in *The Complete Works of Edgar Allan Poe*, ed. J.A. Harrison, vol. 5 (New York: T.Y. Crowell & Company, 1902), 195.
402. *Times Dispatch* (Richmond, VA), September 17, 1933.
403. Personal correspondence with Curator Chris Semtner, Edgar Allan Poe Museum, September 20, 2018.
404. Robert H. Collyer to Poe, December 16, 1845.
405. Poe to George W. Eveleth, March 11, 1847.
406. "Church Hill Is Redevelopment Area," *Times Dispatch* (Richmond, VA), April 14, 1963.
407. Michael DeMarco, "Elizabeth L. Van Lew (1818–1900)," *Encyclopedia Virginia*, December 22, 2021, https://encyclopediavirginia.org/entries/van-lew-elizabeth-l-1818-1900.
408. "A Lonely Life. Miss Elizabeth L. Van Lew, the Noted Federal Spy," *Virginian Pilot* (Richmond, VA), October 12, 1900.
409. Michael DeMarco, "Elizabeth L. Van Lew (1818–1900)," *Encyclopedia Virginia*, December 22, 2021, https://encyclopediavirginia.org/entries/van-lew-elizabeth-l-1818-1900.
410. Ibid.

26. William Gilmore Simms

411. Edgar Allan Poe, "Literary," *Broadway Journal* 2, no. 13 (October 1845): 190.
412. David Moltke-Hansen, "William Gilmore Simms: An Overview," Simms Initiatives, University of South Carolina, http://simms.library.sc.edu/biography.php.
413. "William Gilmore Simms," *Encyclopaedia Britannica*, https://www.britannica.com/biography/William-Gilmore-Simms.
414. Moltke-Hansen, "William Gilmore Simms."
415. Ibid.
416. Enlistment Papers for Edgar A. Perry [Poe], May 26, 1827; *Records of the Adjutant General's Office*, Record Group 94, https://www.docsteach.org/documents/document/enlistment-papers-for-edgar-a-perry-[poe]; Christopher Byrd Downey, *Edgar Allan Poe's Charleston* (Charleston, SC: The History Press, 2020), 106.
417. Byrd Downey, *Edgar Allan Poe's Charleston*, 106.
418. Moltke-Hansen, "William Gilmore Simms."
419. Ibid.
420. Edgar Allan Poe, "A Chapter on Autography," *Graham's Magazine*, December 1841.
421. William Gilmore Simms to Poe, July 30, 1846 letter.
422. Simms to James Lawson, July 4, 1861, in *Letters of William Gilmore Simms*, vol. 4 (Columbia: University of South Carolina Press, 1952), 369–70.

27. John M. Daniel

423. Poe to Maria Clemm, August 29, 1849.

424. Peter Bridges, "John M. Daniel (1825–1865)," *Encyclopedia Virginia*, December 22, 2021, https://encyclopediavirginia.org/entries/daniel-john-m-1825-1865.

425. James Grand Wilson and John Fiske, eds., "Daniel, John Moncure," in *Appleton's Cyclopedia of American Biography* (New York: D. Appleton and Company, 1887), 74.

426. Ibid.

427. Ibid.

428. Ibid.

429. Silverman, *Edgar A. Poe*, 352.

430. John Moncure Daniel, "[Obituary of Edgar A. Poe]," *Richmond Semi-Weekly Examiner*, October 12, 1849.

431. Ibid.

432. Bridges, "John M. Daniel (1825–1865)."

433. United States Department of State, "John Moncure Daniel (1825–1865)," Office of the Historian, Foreign Service Institute, https://history.state.gov/departmenthistory/people/daniel-john-moncure.

434. Bridges, "John M. Daniel (1825–1865)."

435. Ibid.

436. Wilson and Fiske, "Daniel, John Moncure," 75.

437. Bridges, "John M. Daniel (1825–1865)."

438. National Archives, "From Thomas Jefferson to William Short, 8 September 1823," *Founders Online*, https://founders.archives.gov/documents/Jefferson/98-01-02-3750.

439. James C. Jewett, "The United States Congress of 1817 and Some of Its Celebrities," *William and Mary Quarterly* 17, no. 2 (October 1908): 141.

28. John Reuben Thompson

440. Letter fragment before June 30, 1849, from Poe to John R. Thompson, quoted by E.B. Cheesborough, EAPS.

441. John S. Patton, "Biography," in *Poems of John R. Thompson* (New York: Charles Scribner's Sons, 1920), xi-xiii.

442. Ibid., xxv.

443. Ibid., xxxix.

444. Silverman, *Edgar A. Poe*, 352.

445. Ibid., 432.

446. Patton, "Biography," xix.

447. Ibid., xxxi.

448. John Evangelist Walsh, *Midnight Dreary: The Mysterious Death of Edgar Allan Poe* (New York: St. Martin's Minotaur, 2000), 32–33.

449. Patton, "Biography," li.

450. Ibid., lv.

29. Susan Archer Talley Weiss

451. "Marginalia," *United States Magazine and Democratic Review*, November 1844.

452. Rufus Wilmot Griswold, *The Female Poets of America* (Philadelphia: Carey and Hart, 1852), 311.

453. Mary Forrest, *Women of the South: Distinguished in Literature* (New York: Charles B. Richardson, 1865), 310.

454. Frances E. Willard and Mary A. Livermore, *Woman of the Century* (Buffalo, NY: Charles Wells Moulton, 1893), 756.

455. Ida Raymond, *Southland Writers: Biographical and Critical Sketches of the Living Female Writers of the South* (Philadelphia: Claxton, Remsen & Haffelfinger, 1870), 751.

456. *Greensboro (NC) Times*, December 3, 1859.

457. John C. Oeffinger, ed., *A Soldier's General: The Civil War Letters of Major General Lafayette McLaws* (Chapel Hill: University of North Carolina Press, 2002), 235.

458. Griswold, *Female Poets of America*, 311.

459. Ibid.

460. *Southern Literary Messenger* 11, no. 4 (April 1845): 244.

461. *Southern Literary Messenger* 11, no. 12 (December 1845): 752.

462. Forrest, *Women of the South*, 312.

463. Poe to John R. Thompson, December 7, 1848.

464. Quinn, *Edgar Allan Poe*, 622.

465. Poe to John R. Thompson, January 13, 1849.

466. Semtner, *Edgar Allan Poe's Richmond*, 93.

467. Susan Talley to Poe, November 29, 1848.

468. Weiss, *Home Life of Poe*, 185.

469. Semtner, *Edgar Allan Poe's Richmond*, 95–96.

470. Raymond, *Southland Writers*, 752.

471. *Austin (TX) State Gazette*, October 8, 1862.

472. *Weekly Advertiser* (Montgomery, AL), March 18, 1863; Mary Tardy, *The Living Female Writers of the South* (Philadelphia: Claxton, Remsen & Haffelfinger, 1872), 392.

473. Raymond, *Southland Writers*, 763.

474. Weiss, *Home Life of Poe*.

475. "Deaths in Virginia," *Times Dispatch* (Richmond, VA), April 10, 1917.

30. Susan V.C. Ingram

476. "Was a Friend of Poe: Miss Ingram Tells of Poet's Gift of a Copy of Ulalume," *Baltimore Sun*, February 26, 1905.
477. Ibid.
478. Ibid.
479. Ibid.
480. Parke Rouse, "Edgar A. Poe: Small Part of Army History, Large in Land of Letters," *Daily Press* (Newport News, VA), March 2, 1986.
481. Bob Ruegsegger, "Core Mausoleum an Impressive Presence in Elmwood Cemetery," *Virginian-Pilot* (Norfolk, VA), January 15, 2021, https://www.pilotonline.com/history/vp-nk-mausoleum-0110-20210115-drq3iwalurbfllj22yxfmgmprm-story.html.

31. Sarah Elmira Royster Shelton

482. Silverman, *Edgar A. Poe*, 30.
483. John Allan to Henry Poe, November 1, 1824.
484. Edward V. Valentine, "Conversation with Mrs. Shelton at Mr. Smith's Corner 8th and Leigh Streets Nov. 19th 1875," in Thomas and Jackson, *Poe Log*, 63.
485. "Memento of a Lost Love Is Poe Museum's Object of the Month," *Poe Museum*, February 1, 2016, https://poemuseum.org/memento-of-a-lost-love-is-poe-museums-object-of-the-month/.
486. "Poe as a Student."
487. "Memento of a Lost Love."
488. Ibid.
489. September 22, 1849, from Elmira Shelton to Maria Clemm, Enoch Pratt Free Library, 3, https://collections.digitalmaryland.org/digital/collection/poe/id/23/rec/1.
490. "Memento of a Lost Love."
491. "Marriages," *Richmond (VA) Enquirer*, October 27, 1848.
492. "Memento of a Lost Love."
493. Poe to Maria Clemm, August 29, 1849.
494. Ibid.
495. Ibid.
496. "Memento of a Lost Love."
497. George E. Woodberry, chap. 15, *The Life of Edgar Allan Poe: Personal and Literary*, vol. 2 (Boston: Houghton Mifflin, 1909), 341.
498. "Poe's Last Love Remembered," Poe Museum, September 4, 2012, https://poemuseum.org/poes-last-love-remembered/.
499. Elmira Shelton to Maria Clemm, October 11, 1849.

500. Weiss, *Home Life of Poe*, 202.

501. John Evangelist Walsh, *Midnight Dreary: The Mysterious Death of Edgar Allan Poe* (New York: St. Martin's Minotaur, 2000), 128.

32. Dr. John F. Carter

502. Edgar Allan Poe, "Never Bet the Devil Your Head," *Jonathan's Miscellany* 1, no. 9 (September 1841): 1.

503. *Times Dispatch* (Richmond, VA), September 24, 1905.

504. Dr. John F. Carter, "Edgar Poe's Last Night in Richmond," *Lippincott's Monthly Magazine*, November 1902.

505. Ibid., 565–66.

506. "Poe Museum's Object of the Month May Hold Clue to Poe's Mysterious Death," Poe Museum, September 8, 2015, https://poemuseum.org/poe-museums-object-of-the-month-may-hold-clue-to-poes-mysterious-death/.

507. *Times Dispatch* (Richmond, VA), September 24, 1905.

508. George W. Rogers, "Indian and the Pioneer Once Traveled Scuffle Towne Road—Now Park Avenue," *Richmond (VA) News Leader*, May 10, 1951.

509. Ibid.

510. "Poe's Photo Given to Him," *Times Dispatch* (Richmond, VA), February 22, 1903.

33. Joseph Evans Snodgrass

511. Poe to Joseph Evans Snodgrass, October 7, 1839.

512. Jordan Dodd, Liahona Research, comp., *Maryland Marriages, 1655–1850* (Provo, UT: Ancestry.com Operations Inc., 2004).

513. "Joseph Evans Snodgrass," EAPS.

514. John Ward Ostrom, *The Letters of Edgar Allan Poe* (New York: Gordian Press, 1966), 116.

515. Ibid., 122.

516. Burton R. Pollin, "Du Bartas and Victor Hugo in Poe's Criticism," *Mississippi Quarterly* 23, no. 1 (Winter 1969–70): 50.

517. Poe to Snodgrass, April 1, 1841.

518. Patricia Hickin, "Gentle Agitator: Samuel M. Janney and the Antislavery Movement in Virginia 1842–1851," *Journal of Southern History* 37, no. 2 (May 1971): 173.

519. Snodgrass to Samuel M. Janney, September 14, 1847, Janney Papers, Virginia State Library, Richmond, Virginia.

520. University of Virginia, Ingramm Collection MSS 38-135, Box 2[64], Joseph W. Walker, Baltimore, letter to DR. Joseph E. Snodgrass, Baltimore, October 3, 1849, Copy by William Hand Browne, 1 p. Enclosed in Item 360, text printed in Quinn, *Edgar Allan Poe*, 638.

521. Matthew Pearl, "A Poe Death Dossier: Discoveries and Queries in the Death of Edgar Allan Poe," *Edgar Allan Poe Review* 7, no. 2 (Fall 2006): 8.

522. Ibid., 5.

523. Edgar Allan Poe, "A Chapter on Autography," *Graham's Magazine*, December 1841.

524. Pearl, "Poe Death Dossier," 10.

525. Ibid., 11.

526. "Singular Will of the Late Dr. J.E. Snodgrass," *Evening Star* (Washington, D.C.), June 5, 1880.

527. Ibid.

34. Elizabeth Rebecca Herring Tutt Smith

528. Poe to Elizabeth R. Tutt, July 7, 1842.

529. "Maryland Births and Christenings, 1600–1995," Index, FamilySearch, Salt Lake City, Utah, entries derived from digital copies of original and compiled records. Her marker denotes her birthday as October 18, 1815.

530. Jenifer Blouin, "Eternal Perspectives in Nineteenth-Century Friendship Albums," *Hilltop Review* 9, no. 1 (December 2016): 64.

531. Edgar Allan Poe, "Lines Written in an Album," *Southern Literary Messenger*, September 1835.

532. Poe to Elizabeth R. Tutt, July 7, 1842.

533. Silverman, *Edgar A. Poe*, 437.

35. Neilson Poe

534. Poe to Joseph Evans Snodgrass, October 7, 1839.

535. "Death of Ex-Judge Poe," *Baltimore (MD) Sun*, January 4, 1884, 1.

536. Quinn, *Edgar Allan Poe*, 165.

537. "Death of Ex-Judge Poe."

538. "Edgar Allan Poe Connection in Frederick County," *The News* (Frederick, Maryland), October 22, 1975.

539. "Death of Ex-Judge Poe."

540. Ibid.

541. Silverman, *Edgar A. Poe*, 104.

542. Poe to Maria Clemm, August 29, 1835.

543. Poe to Joseph Evans Snodgrass, October 7, 1839.

544. "Death of Ex-Judge Poe."

545. Silverman, *Edgar A. Poe*, 434.

546. Ibid.

547. See Pearl, "Poe Death Dossier," 8–31.

548. Silverman, *Edgar A. Poe*, 436.

549. "Edgar Allan Poe Connection."

550. Silverman, *Edgar A. Poe*, 438.

551. "Death of Ex-Judge Poe."

552. Pearl, "Poe Death Dossier," 9.

553. "Edgar Allan Poe Connection."

554. "Death of Ex-Judge Poe."

36. Zaccheus Collins Lee

555. Edgar Allan Poe, "The Conqueror Worm," in "Ligeia," *New World* 10, no. 7 (February 1845): 100.

556. "Local Matters. Death of the Hon. Judge Z. Collins Lee," *Baltimore (MD) Sun*, November 28, 1859, 1.

557. *Catalogue of the Officers and Students of the Columbian College in the District of Columbia* (Washington, D.C.: Office of the Columbian Star, 1825), 5.

558. "The Poet Edgar Allan Poe," *Pacific Commercial Advertiser* (Honolulu, HI), January 8, 1876.

559. W. Hamilton Bryson and E. Lee Shepard, "The Winchester Law School, 1824–1831," *Law and History Review* 21, no. 393 (2003).

560. "Supreme Court of the U. States," *Alexandria (VA) Gazette*, January 25, 1832.

561. "Fourth of July," *Alexandria (VA) Gazette*, June 18, 1836.

562. "Local Matters. Death of the Hon. Judge Z. Collins Lee," *Baltimore Sun*, November 28, 1859.

563. Edgar Allan Poe, "Critical Notices," *Southern Literary Messenger*, November 1836.

564. "Married," *Baltimore Sun*, June 17, 1837.

565. "Local Matters."

566. "Great Meeting at the Baltimore Exchange," *Catholic Telegraph*, November 16, 1837.

567. "Horticultural Society of Maryland," *Baltimore Sun*, May 29, 1839.

568. "The Star Spangled Banner," *Baton-Rouge (LA) Gazette*, March 18, 1843.

569. *Alexandria (VA) Gazette*, May 18, 1849.

570. Quinn, *Edgar Allan Poe*, 642.

571. Ibid., 643.

572. "Lecture This Evening," *Baltimore Sun*, January 11, 1859.

573. "Funeral of Judge Lee," *Baltimore Sun*, November 29, 1859.

574. Quinn, *Edgar Allan Poe*, 138.

575. Poe to John Allan, May 29, 1829.

576. Peter Carlson, "Tale From the Crypt," *Washington Post*, October 20, 2005, https://www.washingtonpost.com/wp-dyn/content/article/2005/10/19/AR2005101902374_pf.html.

37. Edgar Allan Poe

577. Poe to Nathaniel Beverly Tucker, December 1, 1835.
578. Poe to Phillip P. Cooke, August 9, 1846.
579. Smith, *Brief Career of Eliza Poe*, 100.
580. Semtner, Edgar Allan Poe's Richmond, 40.
581. "Poe as a Student."
582. Ibid.
583. "Chronology of Poe in Baltimore."
584. Poe to John Allan, January 3, 1831.
585. "Chronology of Poe in Baltimore."
586. "Chronology of Poe in Baltimore."
587. Silverman, *Edgar A. Poe*, 85.
588. "Chronology of Poe in Baltimore."
589. "Meet Virginia"; Weiss, *Home Life of Poe*, 77.
590. "Chronology of Poe in Baltimore."
591. Ibid.
592. Ibid.
593. Ibid.
594. Daniel, "[Obituary of Edgar A. Poe]."
595. Silverman, *Edgar A. Poe*, 440.
596. "Edgar Allan Poe Connection in Frederick County," *The News* (Frederick, MD), October 22, 1975.
597. "Miss Sara Sigourney Rice," EAPS.
598. "A Monument to the Memory of Edgar Allan Poe," history marker at Westminster Burying Ground.
599. "The Poet Edgar Allan Poe Dedication of a Monument to His Memory," *Baltimore Sun*, November 18, 1875.
600. "Monument to the Memory of Edgar Allan Poe."
601. *Alton (IL) Telegraph and Democratic Review*, January 1, 1847.
602. Poe Museum, "A Reading of 'Ulalume,' Read by Dean Knight," Facebook, October 31, 2021, https://www.facebook.com/watch/?v=255735939849754.
603. "Virginia Poe Bicentennial," Poe Baltimore, https://www.poeinbaltimore.org/event/virginia-poe-bicentennial/.

DIRECTORY OF PORTRAITS

About the Author

Sharon Pajka, PhD, is a professor of English at Gallaudet University. She is a graduate of Virginia Commonwealth University, Gallaudet University and the University of Virginia. She has a certificate in public history from the University of Richmond. On the weekends, find her in the cemetery giving history tours or volunteering and running River City Cemetarians.